Ecce Romani Language Activity Book III

Ecce Romani Language Activity Book III

Fourth Edition

PEARSON

Boston, Massachusetts
Chandler, Arizona
Glenview, Illinois
Shoreview, Minnesota
Upper Saddle River, New Jersey

ISBN-13: 978-0-13-361095-6
ISBN-10: 0-13-361095-0

18 SCI 2019

Name ______________________ Date ________ Period __________

CHAPTER 55

THE LATE REPUBLIC

Go Online PHSchool.com Web Code: jqd-0001

Activity 55a Reading Skills: Recognizing What You See

At the left in the table below are the sentences found in Reading 55A, lines 6–15, separated into sense units. For each unit choose the best description from the list that follows and write the description in the blank at the right. Some items will be used more than once. One item that you have not yet formally studied is completed for you.

ablative absolute / ablative (time when) / main clause begins / main clause ends / main clause (complete) / participial phrase with perfect participle / perfect participle / relative clause

1	Annō urbis conditae sexcentēsimō nōnāgēsimō quīntō	
2a	C. Iūlius Caesar,	
3	quī posteā imperāvit,	
2b	cum L. Bibulō cōnsul est factus.	
4	Dēcrēta est eī Gallia et Illyricum cum legiōnibus decem.	
5a	Is prīmus vīcit Helvētiōs,	
6	quī nunc Sēquanī appellantur,	
7	deinde vincendō per bella gravissima	*noun phrase telling how (ablative)*
5b	usque ad Ōceanum Britannicum prōcessit.	
8	Domuit autem annīs novem ferē omnem Galliam,	
9a	quae inter Alpēs, flūmen Rhodanum, Rhēnum et Ōceanum est	
9b	et circuitū patet ad bis et triciēs centēna mīlia passuum.	
10	Britannīs mox bellum intulit,	
11	quibus ante eum nē nōmen quidem Rōmānōrum cognitum erat,	
12a	eōsque victōs,	
13	obsidibus acceptīs,	
12b	stīpendiāriōs fēcit.	
13	Galliae autem tribūtī nōmine annuum imperāvit stīpendium quadringentiēs.	
14a	Germānōsque	
15	trāns Rhēnum aggressus	
14b	immānissimīs proeliīs vīcit.	

Name ______________________________ Date __________ Period __________

Activity 55b Language Skills: Participles and Ablative Absolutes I

Each sentence below contains either a participial phrase or an ablative absolute. (Note that commas are not used to set off these constructions in this exercise.) For each sentence:

- decide whether it contains a participial phrase or an ablative absolute
- place brackets around the ablative absolute or the participial phrase
- write the type of participle used, if any
- draw an arrow from the participle, if any, to the word it modifies
- translate the sentence; use a variety of different translations (see the examples on pages 20–22 of the textbook)

The types of participles are:

present active	future active
perfect passive	perfect active (deponent verb)
no participle (**esse** understood)	

The first one is done for you.

1. Multī senātōrēs Caesarem [Rōmam cum exercitū venientem] timēbant.

structure: *participial phrase* type of participle: *present active*

translation: *Many senators feared Caesar who was coming to Rome with his army.*

2. Tōtā Galliā victā, Caesar Rōmam redīre cōnstituit.

structure: ____________ type of participle: ____________

translation: ______________________________

____

3. Senātus Caesarem Rōmam reditūrum mīlitēs dīmittere iussit.

structure: ____________ type of participle: ____________

translation: ______________________________

____

4. Nūntiī dē Caesare ē Galliā cum mīlitibus profectō ad urbem vēnērunt.

structure: ____________ type of participle: ____________

translation: ______________________________

____

5. Caesare in senātōrēs īrātō, mīlitēs ad urbem proficīscī parābant.

structure: ____________ type of participle: ____________

translation: ______________________________

____

Name ____________________ Date __________ Period __________

6. Senātus Caesarī ad urbem appropinquantī resistere nōn potest.

structure: ____________ type of participle: ____________

translation: ______________________________

____

7. Populō bellum cīvīle nōlente, et Caesar et senātus pugnāre parābant.

structure: ____________ type of participle: ____________

translation: ______________________________

____

8. Caesar sē dictātōrem factūrus Rōmam intrāvit.

structure: ____________ type of participle: ____________

translation: ______________________________

____

9. Exercitūs Pompeiī in Hispāniā positōs Caesar vīcit.

structure: ____________ type of participle: ____________

translation: ______________________________

____

Activity 55c Language Skills: Participles and Ablative Absolutes II

Identify the gender, case, and number of the noun in italics and write the information in the blanks. Then form the participle specified in parentheses and make it agree with the noun in italics. All verbs in this exercise are mastery words from 55A and B if you need to check principal parts. Then choose the phrase that is closest in meaning to the one you filled in and write its letter in the blank. The first one is completed for you.

1. Hīs *rēbus* ___*dictīs*___, Caesar ē Cūriā ēgressus est. (**dīcere,** perfect participle)

gender: ___*fem.*___ case: ___*abl.*___ number: ___*plural*___ Equivalent phrase: ___*c*___

a. Cum haec dīcat b. Haec dīcēns c. Postquam haec dicta sunt d. Sī haec dīcentur

Name ______________________ Date __________ Period ____________

2. Cicerō dē *Catilīnā* in Cūriā __________________ dīcēbat. (**sedēre,** present participle)

gender: ______ case: ______ number: ______ Equivalent phrase: ______

a. quī sedēbat b. quandō sedet c. sī sēderit d. sī sedēbit

3. *Cicerō,* Catilīnam urbe __________________, ōrātiōnem vehementem composuit. (**expellere,** future participle)

gender: ______ case: ______ number: ______ Equivalent phrase: ______

a. quī Catilīnam urbe expellere voluerat c. quod Catilīnam urbe expellere in animō habēbat
b. sī Catilīnam urbe expellere in animō habēbit d. cum Catilīnam urbe expellere nōn possit

4. *Caesare* Galliam __________________, Pompeius Rōmae manēbat. (**occupāre,** present participle)

gender: ______ case: ______ number: ______ Equivalent phrase: ______

a. cum Caesar Galliam occupāvisset c. quamquam Caesar Galliam occupat
b. ubi Caesar Galliam occupat d. nisi Caesar Galliam occupāverit

5. Quīdam senātōrēs *Cicerōnem* in Catilīnam __________________ mīrātī sunt. (**loquī,** perfect participle)

gender: ______ case: ______ number: ______ Equivalent phrase: ______

a. *quamquam* in Catilīnam *dīcet* c. sī in Catilīnam locūtus erit
b. cum in Catilīnam loquerētur d. quī in Catilīnam dīxerat

6. *Caesare* in Hispāniām __________________, Pompeius in Graeciā bellum parābat. (**proficīscor,** perfect participle)

gender: ______ case: ______ number: ______ Equivalent phrase: ______

a. Cum Caesar in Hispāniam profectus esset c. Sī Caesar in Hispāniam proficīscitur
b. Dum Caesar in Hispāniam proficīscitur d. Quamquam Caesar in Hispāniam proficīscētur

7. Cīvēs Rōmānī dē *exercitū* adversum Caesarem __________________ cōgitābant. (**dīmicāre,** future participle)

gender: ______ case: ______ number: ______ Equivalent phrase: ______

a. cum adversum Caesarem dīmicāvisset c. quī adversum Caesarem dīmicābit
b. postquam adversum Caesarem dīmicāvit d. dum adversum Caesarem dīmicat

Name ________________________ Date __________ Period __________

Activity 55d Vocabulary Skills: Crossword

All the words needed for this activity are mastery words from Readings 55A and B. Use only the nominative and genitive for nouns, the principal parts for verbs, and the masculine, feminine, and neuter forms of adjectives.

ACROSS

1. having been defeated
6. army (gen. sing.)
7. to make war on, **bellum** ____
12. to be open
14. from there
15. some
16. huge
21. having been put to flight
23. country (gen. sing.)
25. disaster (gen. sing.)
27. leader
29. character (gen. sing.)
30. to establish

DOWN

1. empty (fem.)
2. nearly
3. legion (gen. sing.)
4. class, family (nom. sing.)
5. injustice
8. only (adv.)
9. against
10. having been changed
11. I conspired
12. people
13. to send away
17. to kill
18. afterward
19. to struggle
20. I call
21. river (gen. sing.)
22. to happen
24. among
26. I began
28. twice

Name ______________________________ Date __________ Period ____________

Activity 55e Reading Skills: Analyzing Structure

Printed below is the text of Reading 55D (pages 29 and 31 in the textbook). Do the following:

- underline the word that begins each subordinate clause and the verb or verbs that complete(s) it; if one clause is nested inside another (see page 35 of the textbook), use double underlining for the inner clause
- put brackets around each participial phrase and each ablative absolute, and draw an arrow from the participle to the word it modifies
- write the letters **CI** above each complementary infinitive and draw an arrow to the verb that it completes

Inde Caesar bellīs cīvīlibus per tōtum orbem compositīs Rōmam rediit.

Agere īnsolentius coepit et contrā cōnsuētūdinem Rōmānae lībertātis.

Cum ergō et honōrēs ex suā voluntāte praestāret, quī ā populō anteā dēferēbantur, nec senātuī ad sē venientī adsurgeret aliaque rēgia ac paene tyrannica faceret, coniūrātum est in eum ā sexāgintā vel amplius senātōribus equitibusque Rōmānīs.

Praecipuī fuērunt inter coniūrātōs duo Brūtī ex eō genere Brūtī, quī prīmus Rōmae cōnsul fuerat et rēgēs expulerat, et C. Cassius et Servīlius Casca.

Ergō Caesar, cum senātūs diē inter cēterōs vēnisset ad Cūriam, tribus et vīgintī vulneribus cōnfossus est.

Annō urbis ferē septingentēsimō decimō interfectō Caesare cīvīlia bella reparāta sunt.

Percussōribus enim Caesaris senātus favēbat.

Antōnius cōnsul partium Caesaris cīvīlibus bellīs opprimere eōs cōnābātur.

Ergō turbātā rē pūblicā multa Antōnius scelera committēns ā senātū hostis iūdicātus est.

Missī ad eum persequendum duo cōnsulēs, Pānsa et Hirtius, et Octāviānus adulēscēns annōs decem et octō nātus, Caesaris nepōs, quem ille testāmentō hērēdem relīquerat et nōmen suum ferre iusserat.

Hic est, quī posteā Augustus est dictus et rērum potītus.

Quī profectī contrā Antōnium trēs ducēs vīcērunt eum.

Ēvēnit tamen ut victōrēs cōnsulēs ambō morerentur.

Quārē trēs exercitūs ūnī Caesarī Augustō pāruērunt.

Name ______________________ Date __________ Period __________

Activity 55f Language Skills: Distinguishing Uses of the Infinitive

Decide what use of the infinitive is found in each sentence below.

- if it is a complementary infinitive or used with an impersonal expression, draw an arrow from the infinitive to its head verb
- if it is the subject of a sentence, write the word SUBJECT over it
- if it is part of indirect statement, circle the verb of saying or thinking, underline the subject accusative and its modifiers (if any) once and underline the infinitive twice
- then translate the infinitive only; in the case of indirect statement, study the examples on page 33 of the textbook for help with tense relationships between main verb and infinitive

1. Pompeius plūs mīlitum quam Caesar obtinēre potuit. trans. of infin. to keep

2. Caesar sciēbat Pompeium plūs mīlitum habēre. trans. of infin. to have

3. Proeliō vincere nōn est facile. trans. of infin. to conquer

4. Multī putant Pompeium victōrem futūrum esse. trans. of infin. to win

5. Maximē volēbat Caesar exercitum Pompeiī superāre. trans. of infin. to overcome

6. Rēx Ptolemaeus audīvit Pompeium victum in Aegyptum vēnisse. trans. of infin. to come

7. Auxilium ā rēge petere erat cōnsilium Pompeiī. trans. of infin. to attack

8. Pompeiō mortuō, rēx putābat Caesarem sibi fautūrum esse. trans. of infin. to favor
(**fautūrum**: from **faveō**)

9. Tum Caesar cōnstituit Cleopatram rēgīnam creāre. trans of infin. to create

10. Erat difficile et perīculōsum potestātem in Aegyptō tenēre. trans of infin. to last

Name ______________________ Date __________ Period ____________

Activity 55g Language Skills: Using Indirect Statement

Change each sentence into an indirect statement, using the given verb of saying or thinking. Keep the same tense for the verbs (i.e., a present tense verb becomes a present infinitive, a perfect tense verb a perfect infinitive, and a future tense verb a future infinitive). Remember that any adjectives that modify the original subject become accusative along with the subject.

1. Catilīna cum quibusdam virīs coniūrāvit.

   Paucī cīvēs sciēbant ______________________.

2. Cīvēs Rōmānī Cicerōnem cōnsulem creābunt.

   Nōn est certum ______________________.

3. Quīdam virī cum Catilīnā cōnsilia capiunt.

   Cicerō cōnsul explicāvit ______________________.

4. Ōrātiō optima ā Cicerōne in senātū habētur. (**ōrātiōnem habēre**, *to deliver a speech*)

   Audīmus ______________________.

5. Sociī Catilīnae dēprehēnsī et interfectī sunt.

   Eutropius scrīpsit ______________________.

6. Multī Rōmanī coniūrātiōnem Catilīnae verentur; quīdam autem Catilīnae favent.

   Cicerō intellēxit ______________________.

7. C. Antōnius exercitum contrā Catilīnam dūcet.

   Nūntiātum est ______________________.

8. Catilīna mortuus est et mīlitēs eius victī sunt.

   Senātōrēs audīvērunt ______________________.

Name ______________________________ Date __________ Period __________

Activity 55h Vocabulary Skills: Word Search

Locate each Latin word in the grid. Words can go across, down, and diagonally, but never backward. All the words you need for this activity are mastery words from Readings 55 C and D.

```
N R T N I N J P P E R S E C Ū T U S Q G
Q L Q X F N P W A B S E N T I S W X B L
J Y W F R G T I M X A E T Ā T I S F K T
R K K O L F P E W Y B T C A S T R A F M
X N T R Q Ō Ū Q G T P O T I O R N P U V
M D C M C U H S L R P N C P Y Y D T L W
D Q Ī E Y J O Ē U T U T Z U Q N N N B I
T X K R F M A N R S P M P G C E N N D Ū
C R R L I J B M D Ē P Z V N M X J N L D
O R L Y P P Z K P A S B B Ā G Y V S Ā I
M K G Z K R E Y Z L M H T V T N I E H C
P Z G F K G H R N Z I S M Ī C R R N A Ā
O A D H Ū C O T E W E U R J E E D I Z R
S B R I T K S H V T D Z S N T T T P T E
I R W N L P T G L P K K L E B I H J W Z
T C H T T F I X Ō Z S U A P C J Q M R Z
U W B U H P S G T I V R N Ī L R L M Z N
S C D Ē M N R X B L P Q M Y G Y W R Q Z
Y F N R B E Y R Y J W A R J P C C Q Y W
J G N Ī M F O S U P P L Y V F Z R L R K
```

absent (gen.)
up to this time
of age
more
friendship
camp
having been settled
abundance
to plunder
therefore
formerly
having been poured out
enemy
heir
unhurt (neuter)
to gaze at
to judge
of a circle
having followed
I get control
in addition
I have fought
once
supply
will

Name ________________ Date ________ Period ________

THE FALL OF THE REPUBLIC

CHAPTER 56

Activity 56a Reading Skills: Recognizing What You See

Go Online PHSchool.com Web Code: jqd-0002

At the left in the table below are the sentences found in Reading 56A, lines 1–7, separated into sense units. For each unit choose the best description from the list that follows and write the description in the blank at the right. Some items will be used more than once. One item that you have not yet reviewed this year is completed for you.

ablative absolute / main clause begins / main clause ends / main clause (complete) / participial phrase / perfect participle / relative clause

1	Fugātus	
2a	Antōnius,	
3	āmissō exercitū,	
2b	cōnfūgit ad Lepidum,	
4a	quī Caesarī magister equitum fuerat	
4b	et tum mīlitum cōpiās grandēs habēbat,	
5	ā quō susceptus est.	
6a	Mox,	
7	Lepidō operam dante,	
6b	Caesar pācem cum Antōniō fēcit	
8a	et	
9	quasi vindicātūrus patris suī mortem,	
10	ā quō per testāmentum fuerat adoptātus,	
11	Rōmam cum exercitū profectus	
8b	extorsit	
12	ut sibi vīcēsimō annō cōnsulātus darētur.	*indirect command*
13	Senātum prōscrīpsit,	
14	cum Antōniō ac Lepidō rem pūblicam armīs tenēre coepit.	
15	Per hōs etiam Cicerō ōrātor occīsus est multīque aliī nōbilēs.	

Name ______________________ Date __________ Period __________

Activity 56b Language Skills: Identifying Present Subjunctive

*Beside each verb form, write the conjugation to which it belongs (1, 2, 3, 3-**io**, 4, or irregular.) Then identify the form by using the following abbreviations:*

PI = present indicative
PS = present subjunctive
FI = future indicative

If you do not know to what conjugation the verb belongs, check its infinitive.

	CONJ.	FORM		CONJ.	FORM
1. videat	*2*	*PS*	**10.** dormiet	______	______
2. servat	______	______	**11.** excipiat	______	______
3. serviat	______	______	**12.** appellet	______	______
4. pellet	______	______	**13.** opprimit	______	______
5. moneat	______	______	**14.** velit	______	______
6. cēlat	______	______	**15.** currat	______	______
7. trahit	______	______	**16.** amat	______	______
8. possit	______	______	**17.** tenet	______	______
9. videt	______	______	**18.** imperet	______	______

Activity 56c Language Skills: Forming All Subjunctive Tenses

Decide what tense of the verb is being used in each item and write that information in the first blank. Then fill in the missing form (indicative or subjunctive) in the other blank; keep the same person, number, and voice.

	TENSE	INDICATIVE	SUBJUNCTIVE
1.	*imperfect*	faciēbat	*faceret*
2.	______________	______________	suscēpissēmus
3.	______________	āmittis	______________
4.	______________	dīvīsērunt	______________
5.	______________	______________	rēgnem
6.	______________	verēbāminī	______________
7.	______________	______________	nōlīmus
8.	______________	commōtae sunt	______________
9.	______________	adiēcerās	______________
10.	______________	______________	gerat

Name ______________________________ Date __________ Period ____________

Activity 56d Reading Skills: Gapping

You know that the presence of parallel structures is the key to recognizing a gapped word (review the Reading Note on page 42 if needed). In each of the following sentences, put a single underline below the first set of parallel words, a double underline below the second parallel set, and label each set of parallel words to show how they are parallel. Finally identify the gapped word and translate, enclosing the gapped word in parentheses. The first one is done for you.

nom. *acc.* *nom.* *acc.* *gapped*

1. Omnēs cīvēs Catilīnam, sed Catilīna nēminem timēbat.

   All the citizens (feared) Catiline, but Catiline feared no one.

2. Cicerō verbīs, Antōnius exercitū Catilīnam vīcit. (two gapped words)

   ____

3. Catilīna ex urbe, posteā sociī eius ē vītā discessērunt.

   ____

4. Pompeius prō Senātū, Caesar prō sē pugnāvit.

   ____

5. Pompeium vīcit Caesar, occīdit Ptolemaeus.

   ____

6. In Pompeiī exercitū multī virī praeclārī, in Caesaris exercitū autem paucī fuērunt.

   ____

7. Antōnius gladiō et Cleopatra venēnō serpentis sē occīdit.

   ____

Which sentences in this exercise contain examples of asyndeton (see the Reading Note on page 26 of the textbook)?

____

Name ______________________________ Date __________ Period ____________

Activity 56e Vocabulary Skills: Sententia Scramble

Complete the blanks with the correct Latin word to match the English clue. Copy the circled letters into the blanks at the bottom, beginning at the left; these letters will form a **sententia**. *All the words you need for this activity are mastery words from Chapter 56.*

(_) _ _ _ _ _	to perish
_ (_) _ _ _ _ _	having been compelled
_ _ _ _ (_) _ _	I have gone away
_ _ _ _ _ _ (_)	civil
_ (_) _ _ _ _ _ _ _	to undertake; to receive, protect
_ _ _ _ (_) _	queen
_ _ _ (_) _ _ _ _	to lose
_ (_) _ _ _	cavalryman
_ _ _ _ (_) _	therefore
_ _ _ _ _ (_) _ _	power; empire
_ _ (_) _ _	as if
_ (_) _ _ _	work, effort
(_) _ _ _ _ _ _	having been wished
_ _ _ _ (_)	hunger
_ _ _ _ _ _ (_)	citizenship, state, government
_ _ _ _ (_) _	woman
(_) _ _ _ _ _ _	I avenge
_ _ (_) _ _ _	I have added
(_) _ _ _ _ _ _ _ _	having been defended (masc.)
_ _ _ (_) _	judge, juror
_ (_) _ _ _ _ _	to follow, pursue, threaten
_ _ _ (_) _	fair, just (fem.)
_ _ _ _ _ _ _ (_) _	victory parade
_ _ (_) _	I carry on, perform, do

_ _ _ _ _ _ _   _ _ _ _   _ _ _ _ _   _ _ _ _ _ _ _ _

Meaning of ***sententia***:

____

Name ______________________________ Date __________ Period ____________

Activity 56f Sight Reading

Read the following passage, choose the best answer to each question, and write its letter in the blank. This passage describes some events that took place between 67 and 61 B.C.

Pīrātae omnia maria īnfestābant ita ut Rōmānīs tōtō orbe victōribus sōla nāvigātiō tūta nōn esset. Quārē id bellum Cn. Pompeiō dēcrētum est. Quod intrā paucōs mēnsēs ingentī et fēlīcitāte et celeritāte cōnfēcit. Mox eī dēlātum etiam bellum contrā rēgem Mithridātem et Tigrānem. Quō susceptō Mithridātem in Armeniā nocturnō proeliō vīcit, castra dīripuit, quadrāgintā mīlia eius occīdit, vīgintī tantum dē exercitū suō perdidit et duōs centuriōnēs. Mithridātēs cum uxōre fūgit et duōbus amīcīs. Neque multō post, Pharnācis, fīliī suī, apud mīlitēs sēditiōne ad mortem coāctus venēnum hausit. Hunc fīnem habuit Mithridātēs, vir ingentis industriae cōnsiliīque. Rēgnāvit annōs sexāgintā, vīxit septuāgintā duōs, contrā Rōmānōs bellum habuit annōs quadrāgintā.

—Eutropius, *Breviarium* (adapted)

3 **fēlīcitās, fēlīcitātis,** f., *success*
4 **Mithridātēs, Mithridātis,** m., *Mithridates* VI, king of Pontus
Tigranēs, Tigranis, m., *Tigranes,* king of Armenia
7 **Pharnācēs, Pharnācis,** m., *Pharnaces.* The genitives **Pharnācis, fīliī suī** modify **sēditiōne.**
8 **sēditiō, sēditiōnis,** f., *rebellion*

______ **1.** What was the situation? a. Pirates were no longer a threat. b. Pirates began to threaten Roman ships in particular. c. The seas were overrun with pirates. d. All the seas were under Roman control.

______ **2.** This situation was particularly annoying because a. the Romans prided themselves on their skillful seamanship. b. the Romans had won wars throughout the world. c. sailing was safe only at certain times of year. d. Roman victories had occurred only on land.

______ **3.** What happened next? a. Pompey opposed going to war. b. It was not safe to declare war. c. The pirates decided to organize against Pompey. d. Pompey received command of the war.

______ **4.** The best translation for **Quod** (2) is a. it b. because c. which d. where

______ **5.** The war a. was finally completed but with great losses. b. could not be brought to a successful conclusion. c. was completed quickly and successfully. d. was a success for the enemy but a disaster for Rome.

______ **6.** What happened next? a. Mithridates and Tigranes persuaded the Romans to make peace. b. The war against Mithridates and Tigranes was entrusted to Pompey. c. Mithridates quarreled with Tigranes about the conduct of the war. d. It took a long time to choose a Roman commander.

______ **7.** The following are all true EXCEPT a. Pompey ransacked Mithridates' camp. b. Pompey killed 40,000 of Mithridates' soldiers. c. Pompey defeated Mithridates in a battle at night. d. Pompey lost many of his own soldiers.

______ **8.** Mithridates a. executed his son for rebelling against him. b. was forced into exile by his son's rebellion. c. drank poison and died. d. died after crushing a rebellion against him.

______ **9.** Mithridates is described as a. a man with limitless ambition. b. greatly respected by many. c. limited by his lack of intelligence. d. very energetic and intelligent.

______ **10.** How old was Mithridates when he became king? a. thirty two b. twelve c. forty d. sixty

Name ______________________ Date ________ Period ____________

THE PRINCIPATE OF AUGUSTUS

CHAPTER 57

Go Online PHSchool.com Web Code: jqd-0003

Activity 57a Reading Skills: Read Like a Roman

Printed below is the text of Reading B; but there is no punctuation, nor do sentences always begin with capital letters. (The Romans, after all, had hardly any punctuation and did not distinguish between capital and small letters as we do.) You, like an ancient reader, will have to rely on the signposts built into each sentence in order to determine where the various units begin and end. Each signpost has been printed in ***boldface****. From the following list, choose the description or descriptions that apply to each signpost and write the letter(s) in the space above the signpost. The first one is done for you.*

- **a.** main verb (not introduced by a subordinating conjunction)
- **b.** verb comes at end of the clause and marks the end of the clause
- **c.** coordinating conjunction introduces a new main clause
- **d.** subordinating conjunction introduces a new subordinate clause
- **e.** relative pronoun introduces a new subordinate clause
- **f.** connection word (review the Reading Note on page 30) leads into a new idea

Note: You may not remember what all the words in this passage mean. Don't worry about that. You know enough Latin to think about the structure of these sentences even if you don't know the meaning of some words.

a, b

Germānōrum ingentēs cōpiās **cecīdit** ipsōs **quoque** trāns Albim fluvium **summōvit** **quī** in barbaricō longē ultrā Rhēnum **est** hoc tamen bellum per Drūsum prīvignum suum **administrāvit sīcut** per Tiberium prīvignum alterum bellum Pannonicum quō bellō quadrāgintā captīvōrum mīlia ex Germāniā **trānstulit et** suprā rīpam Rhēnī in Galliā **collocāvit** Armeniam ā Parthīs **recēpit** obsidēs **quod** nūllī anteā Persae eī **dedērunt reddidērunt etiam** signa Rōmāna **quae** Crassō victō **adēmerant**

Scythae et Indī **quibus** anteā Rōmānōrum nōmen incognitum **fuerat** mūnera et lēgātōs ad eum **mīsērunt** Galatia **quoque** sub hōc prōvincia **facta est** cum anteā rēgnum **fuisset** prīmus**que** eam M. Lollius prō praetōre **administrāvit** tantō **autem** amōre etiam apud barbarōs **fuit ut** rēgēs populī Rōmānī amīcī in honōrem eius conderent cīvitātēs **quās** Caesarēās **nōminārent** multī **autem** rēgēs ex rēgnīs suīs **vēnērunt ut** eī **obsequerentur et** habitū Rōmānō togātī scīlicet, ad vehiculum vel equum ipsīus **cucurrērunt** moriēns Dīvus **appellātus est**

Name ______________________ Date __________ Period __________

Activity 57b Reading Skills: You Be the Editor

Now go back through the passage in Activity 57a and put in punctuation, as a modern English text would have it. When you are done, compare your punctuation with that printed in the passage on page 49 of the textbook. If yours is different, decide whether yours or the book's is better. Remember that all punctuation you see in classical Latin texts is put in by modern editors. Sometimes editors disagree about what punctuation to add, so yours might not be incorrect even if it differs from what is shown in the textbook. If you think that yours is as good as or better than what is in the book, explain why.

Activity 57c Language Skills: Recognizing Subjunctive Clauses

Put brackets around each subordinate clause and underline the introductory word and the verb that complete the clause. Identify the marker that shows the type of clause involved, circle it, and write its letter in the blank, then write the type of clause. Circle Y or N to indicate whether the subordinate clause is nested inside the main clause (see Building the Meaning on page 35) and then translate. The first one is completed for you. Choose from the following markers, which may be used more than once:

- **a.** question word introduces clause
- **b.** the conjunction **cum**
- **c.** key word in the main clause (**tantus, tālis,** etc.)
- **d.** main verb of ordering, asking, etc.
- **e.** no specific word in main clause (do not circle anything)

1. Populus Rōmānus Augustō [cum multās prōvinciās imperiō adiceret] favēbat. Nested? (Y) N

   marker: *b* type of clause: ***cum** causal*

   The Roman people supported Augustus because he added many provinces to the empire.

2. Scīmus [quōmodo Augustus (tantōs) fīnēs imperiō adicere potuerit.] Nested? (Y) N

   marker: C type of clause: indirect command

   We know how Augustus was able to add so many lands to the empire.

3. Augustus (tam) fēlīciter rem pūblicam gessit [ut deō similis ā multīs est putātus.] Nested? (Y) N

   marker: d type of clause: Result

   Augustus managed the republic so easily that he was thought to be a god.

4. Augustus Parthīs [ut signa Crassō adēmpta redderent persuāsit.] Nested? Y (N)

   marker: e type of clause: purpose

   Augustus, and the Parthian for were taken from the grass pay, he persuaded the people to their standards.

Name ______________________ Date __________ Period __________

5. Cum Augustus esset prīnceps, multae prōvinciae imperiō Rōmānō adiectae sunt.

marker: ______ type of clause: ______________ Nested? Y N

____

6. Augustus amīcīs multōs honōrēs dat nē ipse tyrannus videātur. Nested? Y N

marker: ______ type of clause: ______________

____

7. Augustus ducibus mīlitāribus imperāvit ut Germānōs trāns Albim fluvium summovērent.

marker: ______ type of clause: ______________ Nested? Y N

____

8. Germānī tam ferōciter resistēbant ut Germānia pars imperiī nōn facta esset. Nested? Y N

marker: ______ type of clause: ______________

____

9. Scīre cūr exercitūs Rōmānī circumventī et dēlētī sint cīvēs volent. Nested? Y N

marker: ______ type of clause: ______________

____

Activity 57d Review of Subjunctive Clauses and Sequence of Tenses

Circle the correct form to complete each sentence, following the rules for sequence of tenses (cf. pages 44–45 of the textbook). Then translate and tell what use of the subjunctive is found in each sentence (a list of subjunctive uses is found on page 50 of the textbook).

1. Antōnius et Octāviānus inter sē pugnāvērunt ut cōnstituerent quis orbem terrārum rēgnātūrus (sit, esset).

Antony and Octavian fought each other in order to decide whowould rule the world.

2. Multī senātōrēs Octāviānum Antōniumque monent nē bellum cīvīle (commovēre, commovent, commoveant).

Many senators were advising Octavius and Antony not to start a civil war

Name ______________________ Date __________ Period __________

3. Nāvēs Antōniī Cleopatraeque tam magnae erant ut nōn facile gubernārī (possent, possint, poterant, possunt). (**gubernō, -āre, -āvī, -ātus,** *to steer, maneuver*)

The ships of Antony and Cleopatra were so large that they could not be steered easily.

4. Omnēs discipulī sciēbant ubi Antōnius et Octāviānus inter sē (pugnāvissent, pugnāverant, pugnāverint).

All the students knew where Antony and Octavious had found eachother.

5. Proeliō ad Actium factō, Antōnius intellēxit cūr Octāviānus sē (vīcerat, vīcerit, vīcisset).

After the battle of Actium took place Antony understood why Octavious defeated him.

6. Cum Octāviānus Aegyptō potītūrus (esset, sit, est), Cleopatra sē interfēcit.

When Octavian was about to get control of Egypt, Cleopatra killed herself.

7. Antōnius ad Actium victus ōrat mīlitēs nē sē (dēsererent, dēserant, dēserent). (**dēserō, dēserere,** *to desert*)

Antony, having been conquered at Actium, is now begging his soldiers not to conquer him.

8. Cum Aegyptus imperiō Rōmānō (adiecta esset, adiecta sit, adiecta erat), Octāviānus Rōmam rediit.

After Egypt had been added to the Roman Empire, Octavious returned to Rome.

9. Augustus erat prīnceps tantae virtūtis ut Eutropius eum maximē (laudāret, laudet, laudāvit, laudābat).

Augustus was such an excellent emperor that Eutropius praised him greatly.

10. Eutropius quaedam scrīpsit ut Augustum (laudāret, laudāre, laudet).

Eutropius wrote certain things to praise Augustus.

Name ______________________ Date __________ Period ____________

Activity 57e Vocabulary Skills: Crossword Puzzle

Write each Latin word in the grid. All the words you need for this activity are mastery words from Chapter 57.

ACROSS

1. I found
3. to such an extent
5. to recapture
8. loyal (fem.)
10. beginning
12. duty, gift, gladiatorial show
13. having been buried
15. to help
16. any
17. peace (genitive)
18. continually, up to
19. to break in
21. powerful (gen.)
24. I carried across
25. I have lived
26. to rule
27. of love
28. just as

DOWN

1. having been finished
2. circle
4. divine, deified
6. common
7. standard
9. to call by name
11. to cut down
14. to fear
20. beyond
22. to die
23. of course, obviously

Name ________________________ Date ________ Period ____________

CHAPTER 58

A Corrupt Governor

Activity 58a Reading Skills

The following questions ask you to identify or comment on various aspects of the grammar and syntax found in Reading 58A. Keep in mind that your goal should be to read in sense units, rather than word by word.

1. Write the words that serve as boundaries for the two subordinate clauses found in the first sentence (lines 1–3).

a. First subordinate clause: ____________________ and ____________________

b. Type of clause ____________________ Indicative or subjunctive? (Circle)

c. What does this clause describe? ____________________

d. Second subordinate clause: ____________________ and ____________________

e. Type of clause ____________________ Indicative or subjunctive? (Circle)

f. What indicator helps you identify this clause? ____________________

2. Rewrite the ablative absolute **Hōc praetōre** (3) as a **cum** circumstantial clause.

____

3. Describe what you see regarding the structure of Cicero's sentence in lines 7–13.

a. What do you notice about its length? ________________________________

b. How is this sentence constructed or organized? What are its main elements?

____

c. What do you notice about the formation of the main verbs (**coāctae**, 7, **exīstimātī**, 8, etc.)?

____

d. Outline the final sentence in Reading A (**Neque . . . relīquit**, 16–19) in sense units. You may use ellipsis points (. . .).

First main clause ________________________________

Prepositional phrase (describes first main clause) ____________________

Second main clause ________________________________

Participial phrase (describes a noun) ____________________

Third main clause ______________________

Relative clause ______________________

Participial phrase ______________________

Activity 58b Writer's Techniques: Expressing Meaning

The following questions ask you to observe and comment on the way in which Cicero expresses his meaning in his speech against Verres. Reread the appropriate Latin and then give thoughtful consideration to your answers.

1. Reread the sentence **Hōc . . . tenuērunt** (3–4). What do you notice about the wording? In what verbal way does Cicero emphasize Verres' transgressions against the law in lines 3–4?

____

2. Identify five Latin nouns, adjectives, and verbs in lines 1–6 that contribute to Cicero's negative tone in this passage.

a. __________ **c.** __________ **e.** __________

b. __________ **d.** __________

3. Why do you think Cicero created the long sentence in lines 7–13? What is the effect of stringing together clauses without connecting words?

____

____

Activity 58c Language Skills: Correlatives

Review the presentation on correlatives on page 57 of the textbook. Then, in each of the following sentences, circle each member of the pair of correlatives and translate the sentence.

1. Tantum bonōrum multī in Siciliā habēbant quantum praetor scelestus nōn arripuerat.

____

2. Multī cīvēs sīve innocentēs sīve nocentēs damnātī sunt.

____

3. Nōn sōlum vigilēs sed etiam multī cīvēs templum Herculis custōdīre cōnābantur.
(**vigil, vigilis**, m., *watchman*)

____

4. Tot simulācra praetor spoliāverat quot in urbe Agrigentō erant.

____

Name ______________________________ Date __________ Period ____________

Activity 58d Language Skills: Relative Clauses of Characteristic

Reread the Reading Note on page 59 of the textbook about relative clauses of characteristic. In each of the following sentences, underline the relative clause and put a squiggle under the verb in the relative clause. Then mark whether the verb is indicative or subjunctive.

1. Iste praetor est quem omnēs Siculī timeant. Indicative ______ Subjunctive ______

2. Nōnne Cicerō est quī avārōs praetōrēs condemnet? Indicative ______ Subjunctive ______

3. Verrēs erat quī cīvibus Rōmānīs nocēbat. Indicative ______ Subjunctive ______

4. Sunt quī dīcunt Verrem scelestissimum esse. Indicative ______ Subjunctive ______

5. Quis est cui possessiō lībertātis nōn sit cāra? Indicative ______ Subjunctive ______

Reading A: *Select three of the sentences from the previous exercise and translate in the spaces below, making sure to number your choices in the parentheses provided. Pick at least one sentence with the subjunctive.*

(______) ____

(______) ____

(______) ____

Activity 58e Reading Skills: Recognizing What You See

Answer the following questions based on Reading B:

1. Break down the sentence **Ad hoc templum . . . impetus** (5–6) into sense units and write out each below.

Circumstantial clause ______________________________

Translate this clause: ______________________________

Ablative absolute: ______________________________

Translate this ablative absolute: ______________________________

Main clause: ______________________________

2. After studying the second Reading Note on page 61, explain why Cicero uses the present tense, e.g., **fit** (6), to describe a past event.

____

3. In lines 7–8 there appears a nested clause. Write the words that define the first clause and then those that define the second clause embedded within it.

First clause: ____________________ and ____________________

Embedded clause: ____________________ and ____________________

4. In the sentence provided below (lines 12–14), underline the two main clauses, draw double underlines below the two subordinate clauses, and put parentheses around the relative clause that is embedded. Bracket the two participial phrases.

Nēmō Agrigentī neque aetāte tam affectā neque vīribus tam īnfirmīs fuit quī nōn illā nocte

eō nūntiō excitātus surrēxerit tēlumque quod cuique fors offerēbat arripuerit.

What word is gapped in the main clause? ____________________

What type of subordinate clause is found here? ____________________

In what tense and voice are the subjunctive verbs in these clauses?

____

Activity 58f Language Skills: Impersonal Passive

Review the Reading Note on page 63 of the textbook. Then translate each of the following sentences by rendering the impersonal passive verb as either an abstract noun or as an active verb in English.

1. Mox ā cīvibus ad templum Herculis perventum est.

____

2. Cum praedōnibus per noctem ferōciter pugnābātur.

____

3. Multīs lapidibus ā cīvibus prōiectīs, ā nocturnīs mīlitibus aufugitum est.

____

4. Omnibus praedōnibus ut ā forō domum istīus cōnfugerent persuāsum erat.

____

5. Statuā Herculis cōnservātā, ad templum ex urbe tōtā ab omnibus concurritur.

____

Name ______________________ Date __________ Period __________

Activity 58g Vocabulary Skills: Sententia Scramble

Unscramble each Latin word from this chapter's mastery vocabulary. Copy the letters in the numbered cells to other cells with the same number to reveal a ***sententia.***

Scrambled	Cells (numbered)	Meaning
LASSISC	☐☐☐☐☐☐☐ (8)	fleet
IŪDUMCII	☐☐☐☐☐☐☐☐ (26 27 33 7)	judgment
SEMTUIP	☐☐☐☐☐☐☐ (10)	attack
REBUMMM	☐☐☐☐☐☐☐ (31 15 20)	limb
MULSIĀMUCR	☐☐☐☐☐☐☐☐☐☐ (28 16)	statue, image
TĒMLU	☐☐☐☐☐ (23)	weapon, spear
TREGNIE	☐☐☐☐☐☐☐ (34 2)	unhurt
SĀSUCTN	☐☐☐☐☐☐☐ (6 37)	holy
SEVRĪSLI	☐☐☐☐☐☐☐☐ (30 4)	of a slave
TŪTSU	☐☐☐☐☐ (17)	safe
SIAPUTR	☐☐☐☐☐☐☐ (1 39 24)	ancestral
DĒQEUNI	☐☐☐☐☐☐☐ (36 14 38 35)	finally
QIATUE	☐☐☐☐☐☐ (9)	and so
NERPETE	☐☐☐☐☐☐☐ (18)	suddenly
VEULT	☐☐☐☐☐ (11 29)	just as
LAUISIQ	☐☐☐☐☐☐☐ (19)	someone
QASMUUQI	☐☐☐☐☐☐☐☐ (21)	someone
QUSUIQE	☐☐☐☐☐☐☐ (5)	each
IAŌ	☐☐☐ (8)	say, assert
MANDŌ	☐☐☐☐☐ (22)	condemn
DREPŌ	☐☐☐☐☐ (13)	lose, destroy
ĪTRNUSŌ	☐☐☐☐☐☐☐ (12 32 25)	arrange, draw up

Bonus: name the figure of speech in this *sententia*:

____

☐☐☐☐☐☐☐☐☐☐ 1 2 3 4 5 6 7 8 9 10 ☐☐☐☐☐☐☐ 11 12 13 14 15 16 17 ☐☐☐☐☐☐☐☐ 18 19 20 21 22 23 24 25 ☐☐☐☐ 26 27 28 29

☐☐☐☐☐☐☐☐☐☐ 30 31 32 33 34 35 36 37 38 39

Provinces are acquired by force, (but) they are held by justice. (Florus, *Epitome*)

Name ______________________ Date __________ Period __________

Activity 58h Sight Reading

Circle the letter of the correct answer to each question on the reading below.

Cicero writes to his friend Atticus and describes conditions upon his arrival at his governorship of Cilicia (southern Turkey) in 51 B.C. He goes on to tell how he helped relieve these conditions and how the people reacted to his actions.

Levantur tamen miserae cīvitātēs quod nūllus fit sūmptus in nōs. Scītō nōn modo nōs faenum nōn accipere sed nē ligna quidem, nec praeter quattuor lectōs et tēctum quemquam accipere quicquam, multīs locīs nē tectum quidem et in tabernāculō manēre plērumque. Itaque incrēdibilem in modum concursus fiunt ex agrīs, ex vīcīs, ex domibus omnibus. Mēhercule etiam adventū nostrō revīviscunt iūstitia, abstinentia, clēmentia tuī Cicerōnis.

—Cicero, *Epistulae ad Atticum*

1 **levō, -āre, -āvī, -ātus,** *to relieve*
sūmptus, -ūs, m., *expense*
in nōs: *in regard to me*, i.e., my governorship
Scītō, *Know*, imperative
2 **faenum, -ī,** n., *hay*
lignum, -ī, n., *(fire)wood*
praeter, prep. + acc., *beyond, except*
3 **tēctum, -ī,** n., *roof*
4 **tabernāculum, -ī,** n., *tent*
plērumque, adv., *ordinarily, usually*
5 **vīcus, -ī,** m., *village, hamlet*
revīvīsco, revīvīscere, revīxī, *to bring to life again, revive*
6 **abstinentia, -ae,** f., *self-denial*
clēmentia, -ae, f., *mercy, kindness*

1. In line 1, Cicero ______ himself indirectly.
a. scolds **b.** compliments **c.** questions **d.** argues with

2. The Latin word that is NOT gapped in the clause **Scītō . . . quidem** (1–2) is
a. Scītō **b.** nōs **c.** faenum **d.** accipere

3. The infinitive **accipere** (2) is
a. a complementary infinitive
b. part of an indirect statement
c. part of a negative command or prohibition
d. subjective, i.e., subject of this sentence

4. Which of the following does Cicero NOT say that he accepts from provincials?
a. hay **b.** firewood **c.** shelter **d.** food

5. The idiomatic phrase **nē . . . quidem** (2) means
a. no, indeed **b.** not certain **c.** not even **d.** no longer

6. In lines 3–4, Cicero claims that he usually
a. pays for his own food
b. stays in a tent
c. does not impose heavy taxes
d. provides housing for all those in need

7. As we learn in lines 4–5, Cicero's popularity as governor is apparent because
a. everyone flocks to greet him
b. people invite him into their homes
c. he is offered land and other property
d. citizens make way for him to pass

8. Based upon what he says about himself in the final sentence, it is clear that Cicero is a(n) ______ person.
a. humble **b.** extravagant **c.** unfeeling **d.** conceited

Name ______________________ Date ________ Period ___________

CHAPTER 59

CICERO DENOUNCES CATILINE

Activity 59a Writer's Techniques

Answer each question based on Reading 59A (pages 69–71 of the textbook).

1. What words in lines 1–2 convey the impression that Catiline is a dangerous man who is out of control?

____

2. Cicero twice uses the word **iste** (lines 1 and 11). Why does he use this word rather than **ille**?

____

3. Identify and explain the figure of speech found in lines 2–4.

____

4. What is the effect of this figure?

____

5. The following phrases contain indirect statement. Write VOT over the verb of thinking, SA over the subject accusative, and INF over the infinitive in each phrase.

   Patēre tua cōnsilia nōn sentīs, tenērī coniūrātiōnem tuam nōn vidēs

6. To an English speaker it might seem more logical to place the participial phrase **cōnstrictam iam hōrum omnium scientiā** (5) after the word **coniūrātiōnem**. What does Cicero gain by placing the phrase where he does?

____

7. In lines 1–2 Catiline was presented as violent and uncontrollable. What words in this sentence express the idea of control?

____

8. What makes it possible for Catiline to be controlled now? (lines 5–7)

____

9. Locate and copy two examples of gapped words, one in lines 8–9 and one in lines 11–12.

   a. ____________________ b. ____________________

Name ______________________ Date __________ Period ____________

Activity 59b Writer's Techniques

In Reading 59B (pages 73–75), locate and copy in Latin the following:

1. Three examples of rhetorical questions (review the Reading Note on page 69).

a. ______________________

b. ______________________

c. ______________________

2. Two examples of anaphora (review the Reading Note on page 71). Hint: one example is near the beginning of the passage and the other is close to the end.

a. ______________________

b. ______________________

3. An example of exaggeration on Cicero's part (lines 2–4).

____

4. An example of alliteration.

____

5. Five examples of the imperative singular in lines 15–19.

a. __________ c. __________ e. __________

b. __________ d. __________

6. Cicero wanted to show Catiline and the senators that he knew all about the conspiracy.

a. Cite the Latin for six details that Cicero revealed about what was discussed at Laeca's house:

i. ______________________

ii. ______________________

iii. ______________________

iv. ______________________

v. ______________________

vi. ______________________

(continued)

Name ______________________ Date __________ Period __________

b. When did Cicero learn about these things? Cite the Latin.

____

c. What Latin shows that Cicero had anticipated Catiline's attempt to murder him?

____

Activity 59c Language Skills: Dative of Possession

Study the Reading Note on page 72. Then read the following sentences aloud, underline the nominative case word(s) once, the dative words twice, and circle the form of **esse**. *Then translate each sentence.*

1. Est Catilīnae exercitus in montibus Italiae.

____

2. Domuī Cicerōnis fuērunt multī custōdēs.

____

3. Catilīna dīxit moram, quod Cicerō cōnsul vīveret, sibi esse.

____

4. Catilīnā in urbe morante, erit Cicerōnī magnus metus.

____

5. Reī pūblicae Rōmānae sunt multī hostēs.

____

Activity 59d Language Skills: Uses of Dative and Ablative

The following phrases, taken from Reading C, are either dative or ablative case. Circle the correct identification, then choose the appropriate function from the list and write its letter in the blank. Some of the functions are used more than once.

a. time when	c. manner	e. object of compound verb
b. means	d. absolute	f. indirect object

1. dīs immortālibus (C:1)	dative	ablative	function: ______
2. mihi cōnsulī dēsignātō (C:4)	dative	ablative	function: ______
3. pūblicō praesidiō (C:5)	dative	ablative	function: ______
4. proximīs comitiīs cōnsulāribus (C:5–6)	dative	ablative	function: ______
5. praesidiō et cōpiīs (C:7)	dative	ablative	function: ______
6. nūllō tumultū . . . concitātō (C:7)	dative	ablative	function: ______
7. tibi (C:8)	dative	ablative	function: ______
8. magnā calāmitāte (C:9)	dative	ablative	function: ______

Name ______________________ Date __________ Period __________

Activity 59e Reading Skills: Recognizing Structure

At the left in the table below are the sentences found in Reading 59D, lines 11–17, separated into sense units. For each unit choose the best description from the list that follows and write the description in the blank at the right. Some items will be used more than once.

main clause (complete) / main clause begins / main clause ends / causal clause
if clause / relative clause / ablative absolute

Now complete the numbers in the left-hand column. Study the numbers in Activity 55a, page 1, for an example. Note that when a clause is begun, interrupted by another clause or phrase, and then completed, the interrupted clause will be labeled a and b. Pay attention to the indents for help with this. The first six numbers are completed for you.

1a	Quārē,	
2a	quoniam id,	
3a	quod est prīmum,	
3b	et quod huius imperiī disciplīnaeque maiōrum proprium est,	
2b	facere nōndum audeō,	
1b	faciam id,	
	quod est ad sevēritātem lēnius et ad commūnem salūtem ūtilius.	
	Nam sī tē interficī iusserō,	
	residēbit in rē pūblicā reliqua coniūrātōrum manus;	
	sīn tū,	
	quod tē iam dūdum hortor,	
	exieris,	
	exhauriētur ex urbe tuōrum comitum magna et perniciōsa sentīna reī pūblicae.	
	Quid est, Catilīna?	
	Num dubitās id	
	mē imperante	
	facere,	
	quod iam tuā sponte faciēbās?	

Name ________________________ Date __________ Period __________

Activity 59f Language Skills: The Construction *is quī*

Study the Reading Note on page 79 and note the variety of ways in which the combination ***is quī*** *can be translated. Then underline each relative clause, draw an arrow from each relative pronoun to its antecedent, and translate the entire sentence.*

1. Oportet resistere eīs quī reī pūblicae nocēre velint.

____

____

2. Audēbitne Cicerō id quod est reī pūblicae ūtilissimum facere?

____

____

3. Sī interfectus erit Catilīna, eōs quī in urbe morābuntur timēbit Cicerō.

____

____

4. Senātōrēs quīdam ea mīrātī sunt quae Cicerō in Catilīnam dīxit.

____

____

5. Quī prō patriā pugnāvērunt laudābuntur. (The form of **is** is omitted here.)

____

____

Name ______________________________ Date __________ Period ____________

Activity 59g Sight Reading

Read the following passage, choose the best answer to each question, and write its letter in the blank. In this passage, Cicero continues to address Catiline.

Quae cum ita sint, Catilīna, dubitās, sī morī aequō animō nōn potes, abīre in aliquās terrās et vītam istam multīs suppliciīs iūstīs dēbitīsque ēreptam fugae solitūdinīque mandāre? "Refer," inquis, "ad Senātum"; id enim postulās et, sī hic ōrdō sibi placēre dēcrēverit tē īre in exsilium, obtemperātūrum tē esse dīcis. Nōn referam, id quod abhorret ā meīs mōribus, et tamen faciam, ut intellegās, quid hī dē tē sentiant. Ēgredere ex urbe, Catilīna, līberā rem pūblicam metū, in exsilium, sī hanc vōcem exspectās, proficīscere. Quid est, Catilīna? ecquid attendis, ecquid animadvertis hōrum silentium? Patiuntur, tacent. Quid exspectās auctōritātem loquentium, quōrum voluntātem tacitōrum perspicis?

—Cicero, *In Catilinam*

2 **supplicium, -ī,** n., *punishment, capital punishment*
dēbitīs: from **dēbeō,** *to owe*
mandō, -āre, -āvī, -ātus, *to hand over, entrust*
3 **Refer**: sc. **rem,** the question about what to do with Catiline; Cicero is saying here what he thinks Catiline would want
postulō, -āre, -āvī, -ātus, *to demand*
hic ōrdō: = **Senātus**
4 **optemperō, -āre, -āvī, -ātus,** *to obey*
5 **hī**: = **senātōrēs**
7 **ecquid,** *in any way*
attendō, attendere, attendī, *to pay attention, consider*
8 **perspiciō, perspicere, perspexī, perspectus,** *to see clearly*

______ **1.** What is the first option Cicero presents to Catiline? **a.** to explain his hesitation **b.** to consider his actions in his own mind **c.** to die with a calm mind **d.** to consider if the things Cicero has said are true

______ **2.** If Catiline rejects that option, Cicero **a.** asks whether he will be able to endure exile and loneliness. **b.** asks why he hesitates to go into exile. **c.** suggests that exile and death are almost the same thing. **d.** suggests that people in other countries will not allow a man like him to live there in exile.

______ **3.** Cicero describes Catiline's life as **multīs suppliciīs iūstīs dēbitīsque ēreptam** (2), which means **a.** after you have undergone deserved punishments I will restore you. **b.** you ought not to be saved from many punishments. **c.** you deserve to be saved from punishment. **d.** saved from many just and well-deserved punishments.

______ **4.** Catiline says in lines 3–4 that **a.** if the Senate ordered him to go into exile, he would obey. **b.** the Senate will decree what he is asking for. **c.** he would not obey any decree of the Senate. **d.** for him to go into exile would please the Senate.

______ **5.** In line 4, Cicero will not refer the question to the Senate, **a.** even though custom demands that he should. **b.** and so follow traditional customs in all matters. **c.** which is different from his usual custom. **d.** because Catiline's behavior is so abhorrent to the senators.

______ **6.** Cicero will make sure (lines 4–5) that **a.** he understands Catiline's point of view. **b.** the senators express their opinions publicly. **c.** Catiline understands how the senators feel about him. **d.** the people understand nothing about the Senate's views.

(continued)

Name ______________________________ Date __________ Period __________

______ 7. The best translation for **metū** (6) is **a.** by means of fear **b.** without fear **c.** because of fear **d.** from fear

______ 8. Cicero claims that **a.** because the senators are not speaking on Catiline's behalf, they approve of a sentence of exile. **b.** the senators are silent because they are too shocked to speak. **c.** Catiline cannot understand the wishes of the Senate because they refuse to speak to him. **d.** Catiline must not speak while the senators debate his exile.

Name ______________________ Date ________ Period __________

CHAPTER 60

Two Rival Centurions

Go Online PHSchool.com Web Code: jqd-0006

Activity 60a Reading Skills: Recognizing What You See

Answer the following questions based on lines 1–5 of Reading 60A.

1. What word does **ferventēs** (1) modify? How do you know?

____

2. How do you know that **fūsilī** (1) modifies **argillā** and not **ferventēs** or **glandēs**?

____

3. What helps you realize that **fundīs** (2) is ablative case (not dative)?

____

____

4. What signals the end of the relative clause that begins with **quae** (2)?

____

5. How do you know that **Hae** (3) refers back to **casās** (2)?

____

____

6. Find examples of the following uses of the ablative.

an ablative of manner: ____________________

two ablative absolutes: ____________________, ____________________

two prepositional phrases with the ablative:

____________________, ____________________

two ablatives of means: ____________________, ____________________

an ablative of cause: ____________________

Name ______________________ Date __________ Period __________

Activity 60b Reading Skills: Subordinate Clauses

Follow the directions given below for the sentence in lines 6–10 of Reading A.

At tanta mīlitum virtūs atque ea praesentia animī fuit

ut,

cum undique torrērentur

maximāque tēlōrum multitūdine premerentur

suaque omnia impedīmenta atque fortūnās cōnflāgrāre intellegerent,

nōn modo

dēmigrandī causā

dē vāllō dēcēderet nēmō,

sed paene nē respiceret quidem quisquam,

ac tum omnēs ācerrimē fortissimēque pugnārent.

1. Put a single underline below the conjunction **ut** and below the three verbs that complete it. (Note that the **ut** clause is interrupted by the **cum** clause.)

2. How do we know that this **ut** clause is a result clause?

Because it introduces the subordinate clause.

3. What adverbs and connecting words help guide you through the three parts of the **ut** clause? Put a box around these words.

4. Put a double underline below the conjunction **cum** and below the three verbs that complete it.

5. What word helps you understand the structure of the **cum** clause? atque
Circle two instances of this word.

6. Now translate the sentence. Do it once while looking at the sense unit version given above, and then do it again using the standard format version printed on page 87 of the textbook. Be sure to focus on the words discussed in this activity when you return to the textbook.

____

____

Name ______________________________ Date __________ Period ____________

Activity 60c Reading Skills: Recognizing What You See

In the grid below, identify each element of the sentence; then fill in the numbers at the left. See Activity 55a, page 1, for a model. We have not given a list of elements this time, but one difficult one is filled in for you.

	Paulum quidem intermissā flammā	main clause begins
	et quōdam locō turrī adāctā et contingente vāllum,	purpose clause continues
	tertiae cohortis centuriōnēs	prepositional phrase
	ex eō, quō stābant, locō	*prepositional phrase with relative clause nested inside*
	recessērunt	main clause continues
	suōsque omnēs remōvērunt,	Subordinate clause continues
	nūtū vōcibusque hostēs,	main clause continues
	sī introīre vellent,	purpose clause
	vocāre coepērunt;	main clause continues
	quōrum prōgredī ausus est nēmō.	indirect question

Activity 60d Writer's Techniques: Describing the Action

In lines 4–19 of Reading 60B, Caesar moves the focus of the narrative back and forth among Pullo, Vorenus, and the Gauls. Summarize in each box what happens in the corresponding segment of the story. The first one is completed for you.

Pullo	*Pullo taunts Vorenus, then goes out from the fortifications*
Vorenus	
Pullo	
Gauls	
Pullo	
Vorenus	

(continued)

Name ____________________ Date __________ Period __________

Gauls	
Vorenus	
Pullo	
both	

Activity 60e Language Skills: The Double Dative

Study the Reading Note on page 95. In addition, note also these words that are often found as a dative of purpose:

exitiō esse, *to be a cause of destruction*

exemplō esse, *to be an example*

*Write the letter **P** over each dative of purpose and **R** over each dative of reference in the sentences below and translate each into good English.*

1. Gallī spērābant sē exitiō Rōmānīs fore. (**fore**: alternate form of **futūrus esse**)

   ____

2. Mīlitēs in castrīs Q. Cicerōnis, ā Gallīs petītī, fuērunt cūrae Caesarī. Sē rogābat quis illīs salūtī futūrus esset.

   ____

   ____

3. Incendia in castrīs fuērunt metuī mīlitibus.

   ____

4. Eruntne hī mīlitēs auxiliō comitibus suīs?

   ____

5. Facta Pullōnis Vorēnīque exemplō aliīs mīlitibus sunt.

   ____

Name ______________________ Date __________ Period ____________

Activity 60f Language Skills: Conditional Sentences I

Review conditional sentences on pages 96–97 of the textbook. Then circle the appropriate word to indicate whether each condition is simple or imaginary and whether each refers to the past, present, or future; then translate each sentence.

1. Miser sum, nisi tē videō. simple / imaginary past / present / future

____

2. Miser eram, nisi tē vidēbam. simple / imaginary past / present / future

____

3. Miser sim, nisi tē videam. simple / imaginary past / present / future

____

4. Miser fuissem, nisi tē vīdissem. simple / imaginary past / present / future

____

5. Miser fuī, nisi tē vīdī. simple / imaginary past / present / future

____

6. Miser erō, nisi tē vīderō. simple / imaginary past / present / future

____

7. Miser erō, nisi tē vidēbō. simple / imaginary past / present / future

____

8. Miser essem, nisi tē vidērem. simple / imaginary past / present / future

____

Sometimes conditional sentences are "mixed," that is, they contain different tenses in the protasis and apodosis, as in the following example:

9. Miser essem, nisi tē vīdissem. simple / imaginary past / present / future

____

Name ______________________ Date __________ Period __________

Activity 60g Language Skills: Conditional Sentences II

Complete the sentences 1–6 with the correct forms of ***dīcere*** *in the if-clauses and* ***crēdere*** *in the main clauses, as the rules and the sense dictate. Then translate each sentence.*

(present imaginary) **1.** Etiamsī tū vēra dicas, nēmō tibi credat.

If you were saying the truth, nobody would trust you.

(future imaginary) **2.** Etiamsī tū vēra dices, nēmō tibi credet

If you would say the truth, nobody would trust you.

(past imaginary) **3.** Etiamsī tū vēra dixeris, nēmō tibi credid erit.

If you had said the truth, nobody would have trusted you.

(simple present) **4.** Etiamsī tū vēra dicis, nēmō tibi credit.

If you say the truth, nobody would trust you.

(simple future) **5.** Etiamsī tū vēra dices, nēmō tibi credet.

If you say the truth, nobody will trust you.

(mixed imaginary; past protasis, present apodosis) **6.** Etiamsī tū vēra dixeris, nēmō tibi credit.

If you had said the truth, nobody would trust you.

For 7–9, use ***cōnārī*** *(deponent) in the if-clause and* ***laudāre****, in the passive voice, in the main clause.*

(future imaginary) **7.** Discipulī, sī hoc facere Conabitur, ā magistrō Laudabit.

Followers, if they would try to make this, would be praised a leader.

(simple future) **8.** Discipulī, sī hoc facere Conabitur, ā magistrō Laudabit.

Followers, if they will try to make this, will be praised a ralea

(past imaginary) **9.** Discipulī, sī hoc facere Conatus sit, ā magistrō Laudaverit.

Followers, if they had tried to make this, would have been praised a ruler.

Name ______________________ Date __________ Period ____________

Activity 60h Language Skills: Conditional Sentences III

Translate each of the following quotations from Latin authors:

1. Sī vīs amārī, amā! (Seneca)

   If you want to be loved, love!

2. Dī nōn cūrant quid agat hūmānum genus. Nam sī cūrent, bene bonīs sit, male malīs. Quod nunc abest. (Ennius)

   Gods do not care about what they do for humanity. For if we are to see, all is well's goods, the resulting evils, I is now gone.

3. Sī vīveret, verba eius audīrētis. (Cicero)

   If he were living, you would hear his words.

4. Dīcēs "Ēheu!" sī tē in speculō vīderis. (Horace) (**speculum**, *mirror*)

   You will say "Alas!" if you see yourself in a mirror.

Name ______________________________ Date __________ Period __________

Activity 60i Vocabulary Skills: Word Search

There are 25 Latin military terms in the word search below. Put each Latin word on the line next to its meaning (see pages 80–82 of the textbook), then locate it in the puzzle. Words can go across, up, down, or diagonally, but not backwards.

T V S A G I T T Ā R I Ī T G L R
G K U I Z S M L B Y T J Ō V E H
R E I M M M C L T A K R D B G O
V A D T Ī P Y Ū D R L K R Y I S
B L A D C L E Q T X H L O G Ō T
L Ā L H P Q E D T U R R I S B I
M C G V R J P S Ī N M Ō K S R S
M S R Ā G A L E A M I C L A T N
A P M L Y G Y X B R E M I A R A
L E T L Q R C R U M U N R R C G
I D E U L J F T U L Ō T T T O M
U I S M J L N N Ē L S G Q A H U
Q T T C Z E G T O A P M J D O L
A Ē U H C I M C C F U N D A R Ī
K S D R S L M Ū N Ī T I Ō R S P
X R Ō W R L L C Y K V B X W W B

__________ eagle

__________ catapult, torsion machine

__________ camp

__________ commander of 100 men

__________ helmet

__________ sword

__________ enemy

__________ baggage

__________ legion

__________ soldier

__________ stockade

__________ rank

__________ foot soldiers

__________ 1/10th of a legion

__________ settlement (of retired soldiers)

__________ sling

__________ pike, spear

__________ archers

__________ ladder

__________ shield

__________ military standard

__________ "tortoise," interlocked shields

__________ tower on wheels

__________ offensive weapon, spear

__________ palisade, rampart

Name ______________________ Date ________ Period ___________

CHAPTER 61

Customs of the Gauls

Activity 61a Reading Skills: Read the Whole Sentence!

You know that it is very important to read the whole sentence before you try to interpret what the Latin says. Listed below are words from Reading 61A whose function is not immediately obvious. Answer the question about each.

1. When do you know how **est** (1) fits into the structure of the sentence?

____

2. **quī** (1 and 2) is an example of the **is quī** construction (see the note on page 79 in the textbook) with the antecedent omitted. How do you know that this is the case?

____

3. How do you know that **-que** (3) begins a new clause?

____

4. What two factors make the case and reason for **administrīs** (3) clear?

____

5. Both **posse** (4) and **placārī** (5) are infinitives. What makes the function of each clear?

____

____

6. How do you know that **-que** (5) begins a new clause?

____

7. What case are the words **eiusdem generis** (5)? At what point does the function of these words become clear?

____

8. In what two ways does the structure of the sentence become clearer when you encounter the word **membra** (7)?

____

____

Name ________________________ Date __________ Period __________

9. What two cases could the perfect participle **circumventī** (7) be? When do you know which one it actually is?

____

10. Perfect passive verbs such as **capta sunt** very often have the helping verb last. Caesar, however, often puts the helping verb first, i.e., **sunt capta.** Find three examples of this word order in A:1–11.

a. ____________ b. ____________ c. ____________

Activity 61b Reading Skills: Recognizing What You See I

Deōrum maximē Mercurium colunt. Huius sunt plūrima simulācra: hunc omnium inventōrem artium ferunt, hunc viārum atque itinerum ducem, hunc ad quaestūs pecūniae mercātūrāsque habēre vim maximam arbitrantur. Post hunc Apollinem et Mārtem et Iovem et Minervam. Dē hīs eandem ferē quam reliquae gentēs, habent opīniōnem: Apollinem morbōs dēpellere, Minervam operum atque artificiōrum initia trādere, Iovem imperium caelestium tenēre, Mārtem bella regere. Huic, cum proeliō dīmicāre cōnstituērunt, ea quae bellō cēperint plērumque dēvovent: cum superāvērunt, animālia capta immolant reliquāsque rēs in ūnum locum cōnferunt.

In Reading B above, do the following:

1. For each example of indirect statement, write the letters VOT above the verb of thinking; SA above the subject accusative; and INF above the infinitive.

2. In the second sentence, a verb needs to be supplied in two of the phrases. What verb? Put a caret ^ at the appropriate points and write the missing infinitive above the carets.

3. In the last sentence, underline each subordinate clause and circle the clause marker. Also circle the word that connects the two halves of the main clause (**plērumque** is not the word to circle).

Name ______________________ Date __________ Period __________

Activity 61c Reading Skills: Recognizing What You See II

Analyze the sentence ***In reliquīs . . . dūcunt*** *(C:23–25) using the grid below. Be sure to indent each subordinate clause by an appropriate amount.*

	causal clause begins
	completion of first half of causal clause
	second half of causal clause

Activity 61d Language Skills: New Uses of the Ablative Case

Review the Reading Notes on pages 100 and 105. In each sentence below, 1) draw an arrow from any of the special deponents that take the ablative to the ablative object and 2) underline any ablatives of description. Then translate each sentence.

1. In Galliā Druidēs erant hominēs magnā auctōritāte quī sacrificiīs fungēbantur.

   ____

2. Gallī crēdēbant deōs sacrificiīs hūmānīs fruī.

   ____

3. Gallī ferē scelestīs, aliquandō autem innocentibus, victimīs ūsī sunt ut deōs colerent.

   ____

4. Deus maximā apud Gallōs potestāte erat Mercurius. Eī erant plūrima simulacra.

   ____

5. Caesar, cōnsulātū suō fūnctus, omnī Galliā potīrī cōnstituit. Ad hanc rem legiōnibus decem ūsus est.

   ____

   ____

6. Rōmānī quīdam Caesarem potestāte suā abūtum esse putāvērunt.

   ____

7. Caesar scrīpsit Germānōs, virōs ingentī statūrā, nūllō cibō nisi carne lacteque vēscī. Fuēruntne Rōmānī minōre statūrā quam Germānī? (**statūra, -ae**, f., *stature, height*)

   ____

Name ______________________ Date __________ Period __________

Activity 61e Reading Skills

Referring to Reading D, page 107 in the textbook, do the following:

1. Locate, copy, and translate six words that have to do with finances or accounting.

   a. ____________ ____________

   b. ____________ ____________

   c. ____________ ____________

   d. ____________ ____________

   e. ____________ ____________

   f. ____________ ____________

2. In the last sentence, locate two examples of indirect statement and copy them here:

   ____

   ____

3. Locate two ablative absolutes that are not set off by commas and copy them here.

   ____

   ____

4. What Gallic customs described by Caesar suggest a degree of equality between men and women?

   ____

   ____

5. What practice shows that men had greater power in society?

   ____

   ____

Name ______________________ Date __________ Period __________

Activity 61f Vocabulary Skills: Sententia Scramble

Complete the blanks with the English meaning. Copy the numbered letters into the blanks at the bottom to form a ***sententia****. All these words are mastery vocabulary from Chapter 61.*

nūmen ___ ___ ___ ___ ___ ___   ___ ___ ___ ___
12 38 28 6

ūtor ___ ___ ___ ___   ___ ___ ___   ___ ___
1 33 40 10

supplicium ___ ___ ___ ___ ___ ___ ___ ___ ___ ___
25 15 35

dēficiō ___ ___   ___ ___ ___ ___ ___ ___ ___ ___
3 20

colō ___ ___ ___ ___ ___ ___ ___
8

opus ___ ___ ___ ___
23

prōdō ___ ___ ___ ___   ___ ___ ___ ___
27 17 37

mīlitia ___ ___ ___ ___ ___ ___ ___ ___   ___ ___ ___ ___ ___ ___ ___
26 5 36 41 14

turpis ___ ___ ___ ___ ___ ___ ___ ___ ___ ___ ___
2 34 19 29

ratiō ___ ___ ___ ___ ___ ___ ___
11 16

frūctus ___ ___ ___ ___ ___ ___
13

potestās ___ ___ ___ ___ ___
24

cor ___ ___ ___ ___ ___
18

cremō ___ ___ ___ ___ ___ ___ ___
30 39 7

fūnus ___ ___ ___ ___ ___ ___ ___   ___ ___ ___ ___
9 31 22 32 4

Sententia

___ ___   ___ ___ ___ ___ ___   ___ ___ ___ ___ ___ ___ ___ ___ ___ ___ ___
1 2   3 4 5 6 7   8 9 10 11 12 13 14 15 16 17 18

___ ___ ___ ___ ___ ___ ___ ___   ___ ___ ___ ___ ___ ___   ___ ___ ___   ___ ___ ___ ___ ___ ___.
19 20 21 22 23 24 25 26   27 28 29 30 31 32   33 34 35   36 37 38 39 40 41

"The disposition of the Gauls is quick to undertake wars."
—Caesar, *Commentarii de bello Gallico*

Name ______________________ Date __________ Period __________

Activity 61g Sight Reading

This passage provides additional information about the Druids. Read it and answer the questions.

Druidēs ā bellō abesse solent neque tribūta ūnā cum reliquīs pendunt; mīlitiae vacātiōnem omniumque rērum habent immūnitātem. Tantīs excitātī praemiīs et suā sponte multī in disciplīnam conveniunt et ā parentibus propinquīsque mittuntur. Magnum ibi numerum versuum ēdiscere dīcuntur. Neque fās esse crēdunt ea litterīs mandāre, cum in reliquīs ferē rēbus Graecīs litterīs ūtantur. Id mihi duābus dē causīs īnstituisse videntur, quod neque in vulgum disciplīnam efferrī velint neque eōs, quī discunt, litterīs cōnfīsōs minus memoriae studēre. In prīmīs hoc volunt persuādēre, nōn perīre animās, sed ab aliīs post mortem trānsīre ad aliōs, atque hōc maximē ad virtūtem excitārī putant, metū mortis nēglectō.

—Caesar, *De bello Gallico* (adapted)

1 **pendō, pendere, pependī, pēnsum**, *to weigh; to pay*
4 **ēdiscō, ēdiscere**, *to learn thoroughly*
5 **litterae**: note that this word in the plural can mean both *writing* in general and letters of the alphabet
7 **cōnfīsus, -a, -um**, *relying on*
8 **anima, -ae**, f., *soul*; **animās** is gapped with **trānsīre** (7) and **excitārī** (7)
9 **hōc**: note that this is ablative case

1. What two privileges do the Druids enjoy, compared to other Gauls? (1–2)

____

2. Why do many men come to train as Druids? (2–4)

____

3. Why are trainees required to learn much poetry? (5)

____

4. Why might this memorization be surprising? (5–6)

____

5. What two reasons does Caesar give for this practice? (6–8)

____

6. What is the most important element of the Druids' teachings? (8–9)

____

7. Why does this have the effect of making warriors more courageous? (9–10)

____

Name ______________________ Date ________ Period ___________

CHAPTER 62

Catullus

Go Online PHSchool.com Web Code: jqd-0008

Activity 62a Reading Skills: Recognizing What You See

Copy out the Latin that corresponds to each English phrase given below. Do not include any extra words.

Reading A

1. let us value ______________________
2. all the gossip ______________________
3. at one small coin ______________________
4. one eternal night ______________________
5. may be able to envy ______________________
6. so many kisses ______________________

Reading B

1. these things individually ______________________
2. no grain of salt ______________________
3. all charms ______________________

Reading D

1. no woman ______________________
2. is able to say ______________________
3. my Lesbia ______________________
4. was loved ______________________
5. No faith so great ______________________
6. on my part ______________________

Reading E

1. that she prefers ______________________
2. to marry no one ______________________
3. to an eager lover ______________________
4. in fast moving water ______________________

Name ______________________ Date __________ Period __________

Activity 62b Writer's Techniques: Motivation and Metaphor

Referring to Reading A, answer the following questions.

1. Summarize in your own words what Catullus is urging Lesbia to do in lines 1–3.

____

____

2. How might lines 4–6 provide motivation for Lesbia to do as Catullus asks?

____

____

3. For what are **lūx** (5) and **nox** (6) metaphors?

____

4. Under what circumstances could an envious person harm the lovers? How will they avoid this?

____

____

5. Some commentators on this poem have suggested this equation:

   unlimited number or uncertainty = life
   limited number or exact knowledge = death

   What evidence do you find for this idea in the poem?

   ____

   ____

   How might this idea help connect lines 1–6 with lines 7–13?

   ____

   ____

Activity 62c Reading Skills: Recognizing What You See

Answer each question as directed.

Reading F

1. Locate two infinitives used in indirect statement: ______________, ______________
2. Locate one complementary infinitive: ______________

3. In lines 3–4, what word is gapped? ____________________

4. Locate a word that comes to the left of its clause marker: ____________________

5. Locate two comparative adjectives: ____________________, ____________________

6. Locate three comparative adverbs: ____________________, ____________________, ____________________

7. What case is the word **multō** (6)? How is it used in this sentence?

8. What form is **amantem** (7)? Why is it acceptable to translate this word as *lover*?

9. This poem can be divided into two parts. Where would you make the break? Why? What words or grammatical forms make this clear?

Activity 62d Writer's Techniques: Tone and Structure

Reading G

1. What words in this poem directly convey very strong feelings? Where are they placed?

2. What words are less strong or less vivid? Where are they placed in the poem?

3. How can this poem as a whole be seen as an extended chiasmus?

Name ______________________ Date __________ Period __________

Reading H

1. This poem takes the form of an imaginary conversation that Catullus is having with himself. Analyze the poem by filling in the blanks.

	Who is being addressed?	What verb tenses are used?
1–2		
3–8		
9–11		
12–18		
19		

2. What adverbs mark the beginning of the second and third sections?

____

3. Would it be appropriate to use the word *symmetrical* to describe the structure of this poem? Why or why not?

____

____

4. At the end, do you think that Catullus has successfully convinced himself to let go of Lesbia and move on? Why or why not?

____

____

Activity 62e Language Skills: Jussive Subjunctive

Decimus, a Roman **adulēscentulus** *(teenager), asks his parents for permission to do certain things. His mother is reluctant to let him do these things, while his father thinks it is acceptable. Tell what the parent says, by changing the infinitive into the jussive subjunctive, and translate what you write. Model:*

Decimus:	Ad multam noctem vigilāre volō.	
Māter:	*Ad multam noctem nē vigilet!*	*Don't let him stay up late!*
Pater:	*Ad multam noctem vigilet!*	*Let him stay up late!*

1. Decimus: Gladiātōrēs spectāre volō.

Māter: Gladiatores ne spectaret Don't let him see the gladiators.

Name ______________________ Date __________ Period __________

2. Decimus: Cisium agere volō.

Pater: Cisium ageret Let him lead the carriage.

3. Decimus: Cantātrīcem bellam audīre volō.

Māter: Cantatricem bellam ne audiret Don't let him hear the war singing.

4. Decimus: Lūdīs circēnsibus adesse volō.
(N.B.: **adesse** has the same subjunctive forms as **esse**.)

Pater: Ludis circensibus adesset Let him be present for the chariot races.

5. Decimus: Ad Forum sōlus īre volō.

Māter: Ad forum solus ne iret Don't let him go to the forum alone.

cisium, -ī, n., *light two-wheeled carriage*
cantātrīx, cantātrīcis, f., *singer*
lūdī circēnsēs, lūdōrum circēnsium, m. pl., *chariot races*

Activity 62f Language Skills: Present Subjunctive as a Command

Catullus is despondent over his breakup with Lesbia. He tells his friend, the poet Licinius, what he wants to do, but Licinius urges him to do the opposite, using the present subjunctive to give a mild command. Model:

Catullus: Volō tōtum diem dormīre; domō exīre nōlō.

Licinius: *Nē tōtum diem dormiās; domō exeās!*

1. Catullus: Nōlō carmina aut legere aut scrībere.

Licinius: Carmina aut legere aut scribere.

2. Catullus: Cēnāre cum amīcīs mihi nōn placet.

Licinius: Ne cenare cum amicis mihi non placet.

3. Catullus: Dē Lesbiā semper cōgitō; miser vīvō.

Licinius: Ne de Lesbia semper cogitoi miser vivo.

4. Catullus: Carmina tua audīre nōn cupiō.

Licinius: Ne carmina tua audire non cupio.

5. Catullus: Hanc rem patī nōn possum.

Licinius: Ne Hanc rem pati non passum.

carmen, carminis, n., *poem*

Name ______________________ Date __________ Period __________

Activity 62g Writer's Techniques: Poetry

Refer to Reading K on page 123 and answer the following questions.

1. Study the structure of each couplet and explain how the second line of each amplifies or reinforces the first line (review "Reading Latin Poetry" on page 119 of the textbook for help).

   lines 1 & 2: ______________________________

   ____

   lines 3 & 4: ______________________________

   ____

   lines 5 & 6: ______________________________

   ____

2. What Latin words make it clear that Catullus is extremely upset by whatever has happened between himself and Rufus? Write these words and their English meanings.

   ____

   ____

3. What Latin words suggest, either through meaning or sound, that Rufus is a snake?

   ____

   ____

4. Using the lines printed below, mark the scansion of this poem. Note that the interjection **ei** is pronounced as one syllable. Also, there is no elision between the words **heu heu** in lines 5 and 6, even though elision normally occurs over an h.

Rūfe, mihī frūstrā ac nēquīquam crēdite amīce
    (frūstrā? immō magnō cum pretiō atque malō),
sīcine subrēpstī mī, atque intestīna perūrēns
    ei miserō ēripuistī omnia nostra bona?
Ēripuistī, heu heu nostrae crūdēle venēnum
    vītae, heu heu nostrae pestis amīcitiae.

Name ______________________________ Date __________ Period ____________

In Roman poetry, the presence of many elisions sometimes conveys strong emotions. Do you think that the poem on the preceeding page would be a good illustration of this principle? Why or why not?

____

____

Activity 62h Vocabulary Skills: Analogies

After reviewing the mastery words for this chapter, complete each analogy with the missing Latin word. The missing word may be the same as or the opposite of its partner; put your answer in the same form as its partner.

Example: femina : stola : : vir : *t o g a*
(Note: In an analogy, a colon is used to express the comparisons, so this example reads "**fēmina** is to **stola** as **vir** is to **toga**.")

1. iam : nunc : : tum : __ __ __ __ (de)
2. rixa : __ __ __ __ __ __ : : bellum : pāx
3. __ __ __ __ __ __ __ : turba : : ignis : incendium
4. trīstis : grātus : : miser : __ __ __ __ __ __ __ __ __ __
5. ignōrō : __ __ __ __ __ : : auferō : afferō
6. dēleō : aedificō : : __ __ __ : amō
7. numquam : semper : : gravis : __ __ __ __ __
8. __ __ __ __ : cōnstituō : : lacrimō : rīdeō
9. proficīscī : in mātrimōnium dūcere : : ēgredī __ __ __ __ __ __ __
10. nūllus : ūllus : : turpis : __ __ __ __ __ __ __
11. __ __ __ __ : caput : : cor : pectus
12. volō : cupiō : : incendō : __ __ __ __ __
13. memoriā teneō : vīvō : : __ __ __ __ __ __ __ __ __ __ __ __ __ : pereō
14. laetus : __ __ __ __ __ __ : : trīstis : miser
15. benignus: __ __ __ __ __ __ __ __ __ : : mollis : dūrus
16. __ __ __ __ __ __ __ : reddō : : discēdō : adveniō
17. fīnis : initium : : __ __ __ __ __ __ : incipiō
18. an : __ __ : : aut : vel

Name ______________________ Date __________ Period __________

Activity 62i Sight Reading

Printed below is the text of the curse tablet illustrated on page 119 of the textbook. Read it and answer the questions that follow.

Deō sānctō Mercuriō Honōrātus.

Conqueror nūminī tuō mē perdidisse rotās duās et vaccās quattuor et rēsculās plūrimās dē hospitiolō meō. Rogāverim genium nūminis tuī ut eī quī mihi fraudem fēcerit sānitātem nōn permittās nec iacēre nec sedēre nec bibere nec manducāre, sī barō sī mulier sī puer sī puella sī servus sī līber, nisi meam rem ad mē pertulerit et meam concordiam habuerit. Iterātīs precibus rogō nūmen tuum ut petītiō mea statim pariat mē vindicātum esse ā maiestāte tuā.

1 **Honōrātus**: name of author of the tablet. A verb such as **dīcit** is understood.
2 **conqueror, conquerī, conquestus sum,** *to complain*
3 **rota, -ae,** f., *wheel*
vacca, -ae, f., *cow*
4 **rēscula, -ae,** f., *small thing, small object*
5 **hospitiolum, -ī,** n., *house*
6 **rogāverim**: perfect subjunctive expressing a polite request, *I would ask*
genius, -ī, m., *spirit*
8 **sānitās, sānitātis,** f., *health*
10 **manducō, -āre,** *to eat*
sī . . . sī . . . sī. . . , *whether . . . or . . . or . . .*
barō, barōnis, m., *man*
13 **pertulit**: deduce from **per-** + **ferō**
concordia, -ae, *harmony, good relationship*
meam concordiam habuerit, *has good relationship with me*, i.e., apologizes, is reconciled
14 **iterō, -āre,** *to repeat*
prex, precis, f., *prayer*
15 **petītiō, petītiōnis,** f., *request, petition*
16 **pariō, parere, peperī, partus,** *to produce, make*
17 **maiestās, maiestātis,** f., *majesty*

1. To whom is Honoratus praying? (1)

____

2. What does Honoratus complain has happened? (2–5)

____

3. To whom should Honoratus' request apply? (7–8)

____

Name ______________________________ Date __________ Period ____________

4. List one thing that this person should not have, and four things that he should not be able to do. (6–10)

a. ____________________

b. ____________________

c. ____________________

d. ____________________

e. ____________________

5. To what types of people might the request apply? (10–12)

____

6. Under what circumstances would the request be withdrawn? (12–14)

____

7. What effect does Honoratus hope his petition will have? (15–17)

____

Name ______________________ Date ________ Period ___________

CHAPTER 63

The Value of Friendship

Activity 63a Reading Skills: Recognizing What You See

Write out the three sentences of Reading A, page 127, in sense units. Place in the middle column the Latin that correlates with the grammatical identification of the sense unit given in the right-hand column. Number the clauses in the left-hand column.

		main clause 1
		conditional clause begins
		conditional clause ends
		indirect question begins
		ablative absolute
		indirect question ends
		main clause 2 begins
		main clause 2 ends
		main clause 3 (complete)
		participial phrase with perfect participle

Activity 63b Reading Skills: How a Writer Conveys Meaning

In each of the following excerpts from Reading A, identify an example of asyndeton, ellipsis, gapping, or a pair of correlatives. Then write your identification in the space provided.

1. Dīvitiās aliī praepōnunt, . . . multī etiam voluptātēs (praepōnunt) ____________

2. Dīvitiās . . . praepōnunt, bonam . . . valētūdinem, aliī potentiam ____________

3. Illa autem superiōra cadūca et incerta (sunt) ____________

4. tam in cōnsiliīs nostrīs quam in fortūnae temeritate ____________

Name ______________________________ Date __________ Period ____________

Activity 63c Language Skills: Relative Clauses of Characteristic Revisited

In Reading B below, Cicero is describing the type of person who would be a good friend. Underline all relative clauses that have indicative verbs with a single line and all relative clauses of characteristic with a double line.

Prīncipiō quī potest esse vīta "vītalis," ut ait Ennius, quae nōn in amīcī mutuā benevolentiā conquiēscat? Quid dulcius quam habēre, quīcum omnia audeās sīc loquī ut tēcum? Quī esset tantus frūctus in prosperīs rēbus, nisi habērēs, quī illīs aequē ac tū ipse gaudēret? Adversās vērō ferre difficile esset sine eō, quī illās gravius etiam quam tū ferret.

N.B. **Quī esset** (2) is the conclusion of the present imaginary conditional clause **nisi habērēs.**

Activity 63d Reading Skills: Recognizing What you See

Outline and then grammatically identify the sense units in Reading C, using the grid provided. (One sense unit is already identified.)

		causal clause

Translate this sentence.

____

____

____

Name ______________________ Date __________ Period ____________

Activity 63e Writer's Techniques

In Reading C, Cicero uses several writing techniques that help him express or emphasize various aspects of Laelius' friendship with Scipio.

1. Tell how the technique that is underlined below contributes to the meaning. What is this technique called? ____________________

   In hāc mihi dē rē pūblicā cōnsēnsus, in hāc rērum prīvātārum cōnsilium

   ____

2. Read through the following sentence, noticing the guideposts that begin and end each clause. Then underline the two main clauses with a single line and the two subordinate clauses with double lines. What do you notice about the placement and organization of these clauses?

   Numquam illum nē minimā quidem rē offendī, quod quidem sēnserim, nihil audīvī ex eō ipse quod nōllem.

   ____

3. Locate another example of parallel or balanced phrasing in lines 1–4 and write out the Latin in the space provided.

   ____

Activity 63f Language Skills: Subjective Infinitive

Translate the following examples of the subjective infinitive, which serves in place of the subject form of the gerund (see page 134 of the textbook). Translate the infinitive in two different ways: literally as an infinitive, and then as a gerund with -ing.

Mūsicam audīre est iūcundum. *To hear music is pleasant.*
Hearing music is pleasant.

1. Errāre humānum est. ____________________

   ____

2. Esse quam vidērī. ____________________ (**quam** = *rather than*)

   ____

3. Ars est cēlāre artem. ____________________

   ____

Name ______________________ Date __________ Period __________

Activity 63g Language Skills: Gerund

Choose the correct case of the gerund and write its letter in the blank at the left.

______ 1. Eratne Cicerōnis modus ______ similis modo ______?

a. scrībendī . . . dīcendī c. scrībendus . . . dīcendō
b. scrībendī . . . dīcendō d. scrībendae . . . dīcendae

______ 2. Ōrātiōnēs Cicerōnis idōneae ______ erant.

a. legendī b. legendum c. legendō d. legendae

______ 3. Hortēnsius multa didicerat dē bene ______.

a. dīcendī b. dīcendā c. dīcendum d. dīcendō

______ 4. Cicerō stilum cēpit ad ______.

a. scrībendum b. scrībendam c. scrībendī d. scrībendō

______ 5. Legimusne ______ causā?

a. scrībendum b. scrībendō c. scrībendī d. scrībendōs

______ 6. Fāma vīrēs acquīrit ______. (*Gossip gains strength as it goes.* Vergil)

a. eundum b. eundō c. eundī d. eundīs

Activity 63h Language Skills: Gerund

Give the ending of the gerund as required by the context and then complete the translation of the sentence.

1. Aqua est ūtilis **bibend**______.

Water is useful ______________________.

2. Plūrimī nōn edunt ad **vīvend**______, sed vīvunt ad **edend** ______.

Many do not eat ______________________, but live ______________________.

3. **Ūtend**______ memoria augētur.

(The) memory is increased ______________________.

4. Philosophus vīvēbat **cōgitand**______ causā.

The philosopher lived ______________________.

5. Carmina **recitand**______ optimē discuntur.

Poems are best learned ______________________.

Name ______________________ Date __________ Period __________

Activity 63i Language Skills: Gerundive

In each sentence, bracket the gerundive phrase, i.e., the gerundive and the noun or pronoun it modifies, and translate the phrase according to its context.

ablative

1. [Amīcīs dīligendīs] laetius vīvere possumus.

   By liking friends

2. Hominēs plūrima agunt [amīcōrum habendōrum causā.]

   to have friends

3. Cicerō opera philosophōrum legit [ad multa dē amīcitiā discenda.]

   ____

4. Cōnstābat Forum locum ōrātiōnibus habendīs esse.

   ____

5. Omnibus rēbus vērē dīcendīs, hominēs plūrēs amīcōs habēre possunt.

   ____

Activity 63j Language Skills: Purpose Constructions

*Change the **ut** purpose clauses into gerundives of purpose. Then translate the new sentence.*

1. Habēbitne Cicerō satis temporis <u>ut ōrātiōnem cōnficiat</u>?

   ______________________.

   ______________________.

2. Cicerō in Forum dēscendēbat <u>ut dē ōrātiōne cum Atticō loquerētur.</u>

   ______________________.

   ______________________.

*Transform the gerundives of purpose into **ut** purpose clauses with the subjunctive.*

3. Cicerō in tablīnum intrāvit <u>ad epistulam scrībendam</u>. (**tablīnum, -ī**, n., *study, office*)

   ______________________.

4. Dominus servum arcessit <u>ad stilum ferendum</u>.

   ______________________.

Name ______________________ Date __________ Period ____________

Activity 63k Language Skills: Gerunds and Gerundives

Circle the letter of the correct form of the gerund or gerundive that completes the Latin sentence according to the meaning provided.

1. Nūlla causa iūsta cuiquam esse potest contrā patriam ad arma ____________.

There can be no valid reason for anyone to take up arms against his own country. (Cicero, *Philippics*, said of Marc Antony)

a. capiendī b. capiendō c. capienda d. capiendam

2. Gutta cavat lapidem nōn vī sed saepe ____________.

The drop (of water) hollows the rock not by force but by falling frequently.

a. cadendum b. cadendī c. cadenda d. cadendō

3. Ipsī illī philosophī etiam illī libellīs quōs dē ____________ glōriā scrībunt nōmen suum īnscrībunt.

Those philosophers themselves, on the very books which they write about condemning fame, they inscribe their own names. (Cicero, *Pro Archia poeta*)

a. contemnendō b. contemnendōs c. contemnendī d. contemnendā

4. Ūnus homō nōbīs ____________ restituit rem.

One man by delaying restored the state to us. (Ennius, *Annales*; said of Q. Fabius Maximus Verrucosus "Cunctator," who wore down Hannibal in small skirmishes but refused to engage in decisive battle.)

a. cūnctandā b. cūnctandō c. cūnctandum d. cūnctandus

5. Nūllus interitus est reī pūblicae nātūrālis ut hominis, in quō mors nōn modō necessāria est, vērum etiam ____________ persaepe.

No demise of a state is a natural thing, as it is for a human being, for whom death is not only necessary, but frequently even to be desired. (Cicero, *De re publica*)

a. optanda b. optandae c. optandum d. optandō

6. Numquam . . . praestantibus in rē pūblicā ____________ virīs laudāta est in ūna sententia perpetua permansiō.

Persistence in a single (and) unchanging point of view has never been praised in outstanding men in (while) governing a state. (Cicero, *Epistulae ad familiares*)

a. gubernandīs b. gubernanda c. gubernandō d. gubernandā

Name ______________________ Date ________ Period __________

CHAPTER 64

A Political Murder (Asconius)

Go Online PHSchool.com Web Code: jqd-0010

Activity 64a Reading Skills: The Storyline

*Here are some statements about the content of Reading A. If the statement is true, write **V (Vērum)** in the space provided; if false, write **F (Falsum)**.*

______ **1.** Milō in mūnicipiō Lānuviō flāmen futūrus erat.

______ **2.** Trībus diēbus Milō ad mūnicipium in quō erat dictātor advēnit.

______ **3.** Rōmā relictā, Clōdius Arīciam iter faciēbat.

______ **4.** Clōdius Arīciae erat ad ōrātiōnem decuriōnibus habendam.

______ **5.** Clōdiō Arīciā profectō trīgintā servī armātī erant.

______ **6.** Clōdius cum tribus comitibus raedā vehēbātur.

______ **7.** Milō per Viam Appiam equō vehī māluit.

______ **8.** Et Clōdius et Milō cum suīs uxōribus iter faciēbant.

______ **9.** Milō comitātus magnō agmine gladiātōrum Rōmā profectus est.

______ **10.** Gladiātōrēs ā Milōne iussī cum servīs Clōdiī rixam commīsērunt.
(**comitor, -ārī, -ātus sum,** *to accompany*)

Activity 64b Language Skills: Adjectives with the Dative

Review the Reading Note on page 142. Then circle each special adjective with the dative case and draw an arrow to the word it modifies. Write the letters DAT over each word or phrase in the dative. Finally, translate the sentence.

1. Erantne servī Clōdiī, gladiīs cīnctī, similēs gladiātōribus Milōnis?

____

2. Fausta cārissima patrī, L. Sullae dictātōrī, erat.

____

3. Asconius putat custōdēs idōneōs fuisse iter facientibus.

____

4. Omnēs incolumēs per Viam Appiam iter faciant; nēmō inimīcus cuiquam sit. (**quisquam**, *anyone*)

____

5. Rōmānī dīvitēs putābant lectīcās esse ūtilissimās itinerī faciendō.

____

6. Hic vir, cum sit ērudītissimus, nōn tamen est aptus docendō.

____

Activity 64c Language Skills: Participle Review

Tell what type each participle is and with what word it agrees. Circle the only participle used as a substantive. If other words plus the participle make a participial phrase, copy the phrase and translate.

Reading A

PARTICIPLE TYPE (present, perfect, future active, gerundive)

prōdendum (2) ______________ Phrase ______________________

Modifies ______________ Transl. ______________________

rediēns (3) ______________ Phrase ______________________

Modifies ______________ Transl. ______________________

facientibus (4) ______________ Phrase ______________________

Modifies ______________ Transl. ______________________

cīnctī (5) ______________ Phrase ______________________

Modifies ______________ Transl. ______________________

euntēs (9) ______________ Phrase ______________________

Modifies ______________ Transl. ______________________

Reading B

PARTICIPLE TYPE (present, perfect, future active, gerundive)

vulnerātus (12) ______________ Phrase ______________________

Modifies ______________ Transl. ______________________

Name ______________________________ Date __________ Period __________

occīsō (14) ______________ Phrase ______________________

Modifies ______________ Transl. ______________________

habitūrus (15) ______________ Phrase ______________________

Modifies ______________ Transl. ______________________

subeunda (15) ______________ Phrase ______________________

Modifies ______________ Transl. ______________________

latēns (16) ______________ Phrase ______________________

Modifies ______________ Transl. ______________________

relictum (17) ______________ Phrase ______________________

Modifies ______________ Transl. ______________________

Activity 64d Reading Skills: Breaking Apart a Complex Sentence

Identify the sense units of the sentence in lines 13–16 of Reading B by writing them out in sequence in the grid below; use the left-hand column to number the sense units.

		main clause begins
		ut clause with the indicative
		cum causal clause begins
		ablative absolute
		causal clause continues
		ablative absolute
		conclusion of causal clause
		imaginary *if* clause
		main clause ends

Name ______________________________ Date __________ Period __________

Activity 64e Reading Skills: Reading for Sequence of Thought

Outline, in English and in the sequence of their occurrence, the series of events that led to the burning of the Senate House as described in Reading C. Use the present tense to draw the reader into the action. Include in parentheses the line numbers of the Latin that describes each event.

1. ______________________________

2. ______________________________

____

3. ______________________________

4. ______________________________

5. ______________________________

____

6. ______________________________

7. ______________________________

____

____

Name ______________________ Date __________ Period __________

Activity 64f Map Skills: Across the Roman Forum

Clodius' house was situated on the Palatine Hill. Imagine yourself as a member of the mob that is parading Clodius' body down the Palatine and across the Forum to the Senate House. Using the plan on page 147 of the texbook, identify the various structures that you see on the way; write each one in the blank at the right.

Caught up in the noisy mob, I am pulled along down the **Scālae Graecae,** where I can see the roofs of the buildings associated with the great mother goddess of Rome, the __(1)__, where the Vestals live, and then the round __(2)__, on the right near the bottom. Down to the left is the pool and shrine, called the __(3)__, where the horses of the Gemini are said to have watered at one time during Rome's legendary past. Nearby is the majestic temple, standing on a high podium, dedicated to __(4)__ and his twin brother Pollux.

With everyone pushing and shoving and trying to keep the body of Clodius in view, the mob flows straight across the Forum, passing the __(5)__, the headquarters of the Pontifex Maximus (Chief Priest), and turns left onto the Via Sacra. I can locate myself immediately because to my right is a large, three-story lawcourt, the __(6)__, built by an ancestor of Fulvia, Clodius' wife.

In front is a long series of porchlike offices for moneychangers and businessmen, an area known as the __(7)__. To my left and at a distance toward the south, I can catch glimpses of its larger and younger sister structure, the __(8)__ fronted by older shops, the __(9)__. The angry horde, wielding torches even at the height of the day, spills out into the Forum and fills the space between the various structures.

As I continue west . . .

1. ____________________
2. ____________________
3. ____________________
4. ____________________
5. ____________________
6. ____________________
7. ____________________
8. ____________________
9. ____________________

Name ______________________ Date __________ Period __________

"Back off, scum!" (Excuse me, reader) . . . I notice to the south the __(10)__, where a young Roman had ridden his horse into a chasm in the earth, making good an old oracle that Rome must sacrifice what she held most dear, if she was to endure. Ah, the good old days!

10. __________

I feel the mob veering to the right between the end of the Tabenae Novae and the __(11)__, whose gates are open in time of war. The political violence in recent years has left everyone wondering whether the gates remain open during a time of civil war. I could see ahead in the distance Clodius' body being swept alongside the shrine and towards the __(12)__, where it is lifted onto the platform from which so many speakers have addressed the people. The emotion of the mob intensifies—the smells of the sweat and the resinous torches are overpowering—and I am again swept along as everyone surges across the __(13)__, the place of popular assembly.

11. __________

12. __________

13. __________

The angry mass bursts through the great bronze doors and into the Senate House itself. I am too far back in the crowd to make it into the Senate and find myself swept along the northern side of the building toward the oldest basilica, the __(14)__, named after Cato the Elder, perhaps the staunchest defender of the Republic, who would be outraged at what is happening in Rome these days.

14. __________

Name ______________________ Date __________ Period ____________

Activity 64g Language Skills: Passive Periphrastic

From the word bank below, select the verb form that best translates the missing word and write it in the space provided.

dēlenda erit	concurrerant	pūniendum esse	concursūrī erant
pūnītum est	concurrendum erat	concurrendum est	referendī essent
servāta esse	referendum esset	relātum esset	servārī
dēlenda esse	pūnītum esset	servanda esse	servanda est

1. Cum pugna orta esset, ut Milōnem servārent gladiātōribus ______________________. (must run together)

2. Mīrābāturne Asconius cūr corpus Clōdiī senatōrī ______________________? (had to be returned)

3. Fulvia dīcit Milōnem ______________________. (has to be punished)

4. "Cūria ______________________!" servī plēbsque exhortābantur. (will have to be destroyed)

5. "Rēs pūblica ______________________," saepe dīcēbat Cicerō. (ought to be protected)

Activity 64h Language Skills: Distinguishing Dative and Ablative of Agent

*In the space provided, write the ablative or dative form of the word supplied in the nominative below the blank. Retain the singular and plural, as appropriate, and pay close attention to the context in order to decide whether dative or ablative is needed. Include the preposition **ā** or **ab** as necessary.*

1. Clōdiō occīsō, Cūria ______________________ incensa est. (servī plēbsque)

2. Milō ______________________ servandus erit. (gladiātōrēs)

3. Sextus Teidius lectīcāriīs suīs, "Ad vīllam rūsticam ______________________ redeundum est." (ego)

4. Optima ōrātiō ______________________ dē Milōne habenda est. (Cicerō)

5. Corpus Clōdiī in atriō iacēns ______________________ vīsum erat. (multī hominēs)

Name ______________________ Date __________ Period ____________

Activity 64i Language Skills: Two Ways to Express Obligation

Each sentence below uses the verb ***dēbēre*** *to express obligation. Change each one into a passive periphrastic with the same meaning; keep the verb tense the same. For review, see page 148. Make sure to change each ablative of agent into a dative of agent, dropping the preposition. Example:*

ablative of agent

Viātōrēs ā praedōnibus oppugnārī et interficī nōn dēbēbant.

Travelers should not have been attacked and killed by highwaymen.

dative of agent

Viātōrēs praedōnibus oppugnandī et interficiendī nōn erant.

Travelers should not have been attacked and killed by highwaymen.

1. Cūria ā Rōmānīs incendī nōn dēbet.

   Cūria ______________ nōn ______________________.

2. Multī putābant Milōnem in exsilium mittī dēbēre.

   Multī putābant Milōnem in exsilium ______________________.

3. Nōnne ā Cicerōne vēra dīcī dēbēbant ad dēfendendum Milōnem?

   Nōnne ______________ vēra ______________ ad dēfendendum Milōnem?

4. Corpus Clōdiī ā senātōre Rōmam remittī dēbet.

   Corpus Clōdiī ______________ Rōmam ______________

   ______________.

5. Eī ā quibus iter per Viam Appiam perficī dēbet sint incolumēs.

   Eī ______________ iter per Viam Appiam ______________ sint incolumēs.

Name ______________________________ Date __________ Period ____________

Activity 64j Sight Reading

In the matter of Clodius' murder, Asconius records the allegations of Quintus Metellus Scipio, one of Milo's rivals for the consulship of 52 B.C.

Ibi P. Clōdium tribus vulneribus acceptīs Bovillās perlātum; tabernam in quam perfūgerat expugnātam ā Milōne; sēmianimem Clōdium extrāctum . . . in Viā Appiā occīsum esse ānulumque eius eī morientī extrāctum. Deinde Milōnem, cum scīret in Albānō parvulum fīlium Clōdī esse, vēnisse ad vīllam et, cum puer ante subtrāctus esset, ex servō Halicōre quaestiōnem ita habuisse ut eum articulātim cōnsecrāret; vīlicum ad duōs praetereā servōs iugulāsse.

—Asconius, *Orationem in Milonianum Ciceronis*

1 **P. Clōdium . . . perlātum (esse)**: a continuation of Metellus' previous testimony (not given here) which Asconius gives in a series of indirect statements
2 **sēmianimis, -is, -e,** *half alive*
3 **ānulus, -i,** m., ring worn by those of the senatorial class
4 **parvulus, -a, -um,** *very small*
5 **ante,** adv., *beforehand*
Halicor, Halicōris, m., a slave of Clodius
6 **quaestiōnem habēre,** *to interrogate*
articulātim, adv., *limb from limb*
cōnsecrō, -āre, -āvī, -ātus, *to doom to destruction; execute, murder*
7 **iugulō, -āre, -āvī, -ātus,** *to strangle*
iugulāsse: = **iugulāvisse**

Answer in English the following questions on the passage above. As you do so, compare Metellus' account of the murder of Clodius with that given by Asconius himself in Reading B. Consider the additional allegations that Metellus makes.

1. In what condition was Clodius when he was taken to Bovillae?

____

2. What happened at the inn into which Clodius had been taken?

____

3. How is Clodius described having been taken from the inn? Cite and translate the Latin.

____

4. Where was he actually killed?

____

Name ____________________ Date __________ Period __________

5. Translate **(Metellus dīcēbat) ānulum eī morientī extrāctum (esse).** (3)

____

6. Why did Milo go to Clodius' villa in the Alban hills?

____

7. Why wasn't the boy to be found at the villa?

____

8. What two things happened to Halicor?

a. ____________________

b. ____________________

9. For what other crimes was Milo responsible, according to Metellus?

____

10. Of what three infinitives is **Milōnem** (4) the subject?

____

11. Write out the boundary words of (a) a result clause and (b) a causal clause.

a. ____________________ **b.** ____________________

12. Do you believe Metellus' allegations? If not, what reason could he have for making them? How would the jury react to this information? Why?

____

____

____

____

____

Name ______________________ Date ________ Period __________

CHAPTER 65

A POLITICAL MURDER (CICERO)

Go Online PHSchool.com Web Code: jqd-0011

Activity 65a Writer's Techniques: Cicero's Oratory I

In Reading A, Cicero brings up three different points to support his contention that Clodius deliberately planned to ambush Milo on the Appian Way and that therefore his client Milo was only guilty of self-defense in killing Clodius.

(1) Describe each of the points that Cicero makes.

(2) Write out the subjunctive clause that Cicero uses in expressing each of these points and identify its type.

Point 1 (lines 1–2): ______________________

____

Subjunctive clause: ______________________

Point 2 (lines 3–4): ______________________

Subjunctive clause: ______________________

Point 3 (lines 5–7): ______________________

____

Subjunctive clause: ______________________

____

Activity 65b Reading Skills: Parallel Structure

The Reading Note on page 153 describes a rhetorical figure known as parallelism. Do the following activities for Reading B to help you to understand this figure.

(1) Write out the Latin that is parallel (referred to in the Reading Note)

(2) Indicate what other figure of speech is used to describe effectively the two baggage trains as they moved along the road

(3) Briefly explain how Cicero uses the contrast brought by the parallel structure to the advantage of his client, i.e., to suggest that it was Clodius, and not his client Milo, who was prepared for violence

(4) Locate and write out the Latin of another example of parallelism in Reading C

Name ______________________ Date __________ Period __________

(1) Clodius' travel party ______________________

____

Milo's travel party ______________________

(2) Additional figure of speech: ______________________

(3) ______________________

____

____

____

____

____

(4) Another example of parallelism ______________________

____

Activity 65c Writer's Techniques: Cicero's Oratory II

If Reading C were made into a movie, it might consist of a series of short scenes, with the action moving quickly from one scene to the next in order to show how the attack happened. (Note the short phrases and clauses in the Latin that interrupt each other.) Indicate how such a movie might be arranged by identifying each "scene" in Reading C. Cite the line number(s) of each.

1. ______________________

2. ______________________

3. ______________________

4. ______________________

5. ______________________

6. ______________________

Name ______________________ Date __________ Period ____________

Activity 65d Reading Skills: Breaking Apart a Complex Sentence

Identify the key sense units in the sentence that comprises Reading D by doing the following:

- Underline all elements of the main clause with a double line
- Underline all subordinate clauses with a single line (do not underline **ut factum est**)
- Put parentheses around gerundive phrases
- Put square brackets around ablative absolutes

Ex quibus servīs quī animō fidēlī in dominum et praesentī fuērunt, partim occīsī sunt, partim, cum ad raedam pugnārī vidērent, dominō succurrere prohibērentur, Milōnem occīsum et ex ipsō Clōdiō audīrent et rē vērā putārent, fēcērunt id servī Milōnis—dīcam enim apertē nōn dērīvandī crīminis causā, sed ut factum est—nec imperante nec sciente nec praesente dominō, quod suōs quisque servōs in tālī rē facere voluisset.

If you have completed this activity correctly, there is only one section of the sentence not underlined. What seems to be the function of this section, which is not grammatically connected to the rest of the sentence? How is this section separated from the rest of the sentence?

____

____

____

Activity 65e Language Skills: Indefinite Pronouns and Adjectives I

Review the presentation on indefinite pronouns and adjectives on pages 160–161. Then select from the pool below the form that correctly completes each sentence and then write it in the space provided. No form may be used more than once; some will not be used. Consult the form chart provided on page 324 of the texbook, as needed.

aliquid	quemque	quisque	aliquis	quidem	cuiquam
quōsquam	quaedam	quōsquam	quīdam	aliquō	quisquis

1. Cicerō ______________ (each) iūdicem Milōnem absolvere volēbat.

2. Fēcērunt id servī Milōnis quod suōs ______________ (each person) servōs in tālī rē facere voluisset.

3. Imperāvitne Milō servīs suīs ut ______________ (anything) agerent?

4. Cicerō nōn dīxit Milōnem ______________________ gladiātōrēs habēre.
(any)

5. ______________________ amat, valeat; pereat quī nescit amāre! (Pompeiian wall graffito)
(Whoever)

6. ______________________ remedia graviōra perīculīs sunt.
(Certain)

7. ______________________ aliquid dē ______________________ dīcere potest.
(Anyone) (anybody)

8. ______________________ ex servīs Milōnis fortiter pugnāvērunt.
(Some)

Activity 65f Language Skills: Indefinite Pronouns and Adjectives II

Answer the following questions about the quotation from Ennius on page 160 of the textbook.

1. Write out this sentence in English word order to clarify the function of each pronoun.

____

____

2. What two different indefinite pronouns are used? (Give the nominative singular form.)

 a. ______________________, which means ______________________ and

 b. ______________________, which means ______________________.

3. Why is **dēbēre** an infinitive in this sentence?

____

4. What is the mood of **neget**, indicative or subjunctive? Why?

____

5. **Conveniat** is an example of a use of the subjunctive as a main verb, which is known as

______________________. (See pages 117–118 in the textbook.)

Name ______________________________ Date __________ Period __________

Activity 65g Sight Reading

Cicero comments on the burning of the Senate House.

Quō quid miserius, quid ācerbius, quid luctuōsius vīdimus? Templum sānctitātis, amplitūdinis, mentis, cōnsiliī pūblicī, caput urbis, āram sociōrum, portum omnium gentium, sēdem ex ūniversō populō concessam ūnī ōrdinī, īnflammārī, exscindī, fūnestārī! Neque id fierī ā multitūdine imperītā, quamquam esset miserum id ipsum, sed ab ūnō? Quī cum tantum ausus sit ustor prō mortuō, quid signifer prō vīvō nōn ausus? In Cūriam potissimum abiēcit, ut eam mortuus incenderet, quam vīvus ēverterat.

—Cicero, *Pro Milone*

1 **Quō:** *Than this,* i.e., the torching of the Senate House
ācerbus, -a, -um, *bitter, painful*
luctuōsus, -a, -um, *lamentable*
2 **amplitūdō, amplitūdinis,** f., *grandeur, majesty*
āra, -ae, f., *altar; place of refuge, sanctuary*
3 **concessam**: from **concēdō,** *to give to*
ūnī ōrdinī: i.e., the senatorial order
4 **fūnestō, -āre, -āvī, -ātus,** *to defile, pollute with death*
id: the destruction of the Senate House
imperītus, -a, -um, *ignorant*
5 **ab ūnō**: Sextus Clodius, who started the fire; see 64C:27.
ustor, ustōris, m., *body-, corpse-burner*
signifer, signiferī, m., *a standard-bearer*
6 **potissimum,** adv., *above all, of all places*
abiēcit: understand something like **corpus Clōdiī** as the object

Vērum aut Falsum? *Write **V** or **F** in the space provided. If the statement is false, correct it so that it matches what is stated in the passage.*

______ **1.** The repetition of the word **quid** in line 1 suggests that Cicero has some doubt about his feelings regarding the burning of the Senate House.

______ **2.** Lines 1–3 indicate that Romans revered the Senate House as the center of affairs for the Roman world.

______ **3.** In the phrase **sēdem ex ūniversō populō concessam ūnī ōrdinī** (3), Cicero suggests that the Senate House was a place for senators and people to meet.

______ **4.** In his delivery of the words **īnflammārī, exscindī,** and **fūnestārī**, Cicero's voice most likely grew louder and more passionate.

______ **5.** The clause **quamquam esset miserum id ipsum** (4) is translated correctly as *although that in itself had been heart-breaking.*

______ **6.** Cicero seems most upset because it was an ignorant mob that had destroyed the Senate House.

______ **7.** The body of Clodius was dragged into the Senate House.

______ **8.** The subject of **incenderet** (6) is Clodius.

______ **9.** The pronoun **quam** (6) refers to the Senate House.

______ **10.** The words **mortuus incenderet . . . vīvus ēverterat** (6) make a chiasmus.

Name ______________________ Date ________ Period ____________

CHAPTER 66

Eyewitness to Civil War

Activity 66a Reading Skills: Making Sense of a Sentence

A. *Outline Reading A, lines 3–7, in sense units, using the grid below. Remember to indent each subordinate clause. Then translate each sentence by sense units.*

Name ______________________ Date __________ Period __________

B. *In the sentence above, locate and write out the Latin of each of the following forms and constructions.*

1. future passive participle ______________________
2. passive periphrastic ______________________
3. future active participle ______________________
4. conditional clauses ______________________

____

5. result clause ______________________
6. **cum** circumstantial clause ______________________
7. indirect question ______________________
8. two fear clauses ______________________

____

C. *Locate the sentence containing a fear clause in lines 8–14, write out the sentence in the space below, and then translate it.*

____

____

Activity 66b Language Skills: Fear Clauses

Review the Reading Note about fear clauses on page 162 and then complete the following activity. Read through the Latin sentence and circle the expression of fear (it might be a verb or a noun). Then translate the sentence.

1. Verēturne Cicerō nē Caesar Rōmam dīreptūrus sit?

____

2. "Timeō ut ūtilis sim," gemuit Tullia.

____

3. Erat multum timōris nē famēs in urbe futūra esset.

____

4. "Metuimus ut, cum velīmus, nōbīs ex urbe exīre liceat," scrīpserat Terentia.

____

5. Cicerō timēbat ut uxor ex amīcīs auxilium peteret.

____

Name ______________________ Date __________ Period ____________

Activity 66c Language Skills: Interpreting *Ut*

*Review various uses of **ut** in the Reading Note on page 165 of the textbook. For each sentence, underline the **ut** clause once and double underline the guideword that precedes and anticipates the **ut** clause. (Remember that a purpose clause does not have such a word, nor does an **ut** clause with the indicative.) Use a squiggly line if there is a second **ut** clause in the sentence. Then identify the type of clause(s) by placing the appropriate letter(s) in the space provided at the end of the sentence and translate the entire sentence.*

A. Result	*C. Fear*	*E. With the indicative*
B. Indirect Command	*D. Purpose*	

1. Persuāsitne Cicerō uxōrī fīliaeque suae ut Rōmae manērent? ______

____

2. Multī Rōmānī verēntur nē Caesar urbī noceat. ______

____

3. Cicerō, ut omnēs sciunt, ad mīlitēs conscrībendōs Capuam iter fēcit. (**cōnscrībō, cōnscrībere,** *to enlist, recruit*) ______

____

4. Adeō Cicerō fīlium suum Mārcum amābat ut iūvenem sēcum nē ā Caesare caperētur duceret. ______

____

____

5. Terentia tam sollicita est ut multās epistulās ad virum suum scrībat. ______

____

6. Multī metuēbant nē famēs in urbe esset. ______

____

7. Cum Cicerō ē Romā discēderet, monuit servōs suōs nē eīs aufugiendum esset. ______

____

8. Cicerō ad Tulliam epistulam scrīpsit nē timēret. ______

____

Name ______________________________ Date __________ Period ____________

Activity 66d Language Skills: Questions in Latin

Each of the following sentences contains a question of some kind: deliberative (page 166), direct, indirect, or rhetorical (page 69). Translate each and then, considering whether the verb of the question is indicative (direct, rhetorical) or subjunctive (deliberative, indirect), identify the type of question in each of the following sentences.

1. Quid dīcam? Quid faciam?

Translation ______________________________

Type ______________________________

2. Num Pompeius ā Caesare vincētur?

Translation ______________________________

Type ______________________________

3. Quid facerem?

Translation ______________________________

Type ______________________________

4. Cicerō mīrātur quid scriptūrus sit.

Translation ______________________________

Type ______________________________

5. Discēdāmus?

Translation ______________________________

Type ______________________________

6. Moriēmurne aut vīvēmus?

Translation ______________________________

Type ______________________________

7. Faventne dī Caesarī vel Pompeiō magis?

Translation ______________________________

Type ______________________________

8. Quod cōnsilium capiās?

Translation ______________________________

Type ______________________________

Name ______________________________ Date __________ Period ____________

Activity 66e Reading for Analysis I: Cicero's Dilemma

What aspects of Reading B indicate that Cicero is hesitant about what to do and whom to follow, now that civil war has broken out? Explain or elaborate upon those listed below.

1. What does Cicero's reference to Caesar as **istīus** (2) and **istī** (4) suggest about his feelings toward the general?

____

____

2. **Ego quid agam? Eum persequar? Trādam igitur istī mē?** (3–4) What type of question is used in these sentences? How do they reveal Cicero's hesitancy?

____

____

3. His feelings about Pompey: **Dē Pompeiō sciō nihil** (2–3) and **ubi sit nesciō?** (4)

____

____

4. His feelings about Caesar: **Num (mē trādere possum) etiam honestē? Nūllō modō.** (5)

____

____

5. Cicero's general bewilderment: **Explicārī rēs nōn potest.** (6)

____

____

Name ______________________ Date __________ Period __________

Activity 66f Reading for Analysis II: Pompey and Caesar

Compare and contrast the letters of Pompey and Caesar to Cicero (Readings C and D) by answering the following questions. Justify your observations by citing the appropriate Latin.

1. How are Letters B and C similar? Find six similarities.

a. ______________________________

____

b. ______________________________

____

c. ______________________________

____

d. ______________________________

____

e. ______________________________

____

f. ______________________________

____

2. What is the main difference?

____

____

____

____

____

____

Name ______________________________ Date __________ Period ____________

Activity 66g Sight Reading

Caesar explains why he left his province of Gaul to invade Italy. He is addressing Lentulus Spinther, who commanded the forces of Pompey at Corfinium, east of Rome. Lentulus, forced to surrender, was begging Caesar for his life.

Caesar interpellat sē nōn maleficiī causā ex prōvinciā ēgressum, sed utī sē ā contumēliīs inimīcōrum dēfenderet, ut tribūnōs plēbis in eā rē ex cīvitāte expulsōs in suam dignitātem restitueret, ut sē et populum Rōmānum factiōne paucōrum oppressum in lībertātem vindicāret. Cuius ōrātiōne cōnfirmātus Lentulus, ut in oppidum revertī liceat, petit: quod dē suā salūte impetrāverit, fore etiam reliquīs ad suam spem sōlāciō; adeō esse perterritōs nōnnūllōs, ut suae vītae dūrius cōnsulere cōgantur. Factā potestāte discēdit.

—Caesar, *Bellum civile*

1 **maleficium, -ī**, n., *mischief, crime, wrongdoing*
ēgressum: = **ēgressum (esse)**
utī: = **ut**
contumēlia, -ae, f. *insult, slander*
2 **in eā rē**: *with regard to his situation, in support of his cause*
dignitās, dignitātis, f., *honor, esteem, status*
3 **in lībertātem vindicāre**, *to restore to freedom, liberate*
4 **oppidum, -ī**, n., *town*; here, Corfinium
5 **impetrō, -āre, -āvī, -ātus**, *to gain one's request*
fore: = **futūrum esse. Fore** and **esse** (6) are infinitives in indirect statement with a verb such as **dīcit** understood.
reliquīs . . . sōlāciō: *comfort to the others*, lit., *for a comfort for the others*; double dative
6 **suae vītae dūrius cōnsulere**, *to consider doing themselves violence*, lit., *to consider (treating their own lives) more harshly*

Answer each question as ***V*** *(****Vērum****, True) or* ***F*** *(****Falsum****, False). Correct those which are false, basing your answers on the Latin text.*

______ **1.** Caesar left his province in order to destroy his political opponents.

____

______ **2.** The clause **utī . . . dēfenderet** (1–2) may be translated *to defend.*

____

______ **3.** Caesar hoped that the tribunes of the people would restore him to his former status.

____

(continued)

Name ______________________________ Date __________ Period ____________

______ **4.** The past participle **oppressum** (3) modifies the pronoun **sē**.

____

______ **5.** Caesar was trying to free the Roman people from the domination of a small clique.

____

______ **6.** The relative pronoun **Cuius** (4) refers to **lībertātem**.

____

______ **7.** Lentulus asked that he be allowed to leave Corfinium. (4–5)

____

______ **8.** The clause **ut . . . liceat** (4) is a result clause.

____

______ **9.** Lentulus believed that Caesar's leniency would bring others hope. (5)

____

______ **10.** Lentulus says it was Caesar's plan to force his enemies to take their own lives.

____

______ **11.** The clause **ut . . . cōgantur** (6) is an indirect command.

____

______ **12.** Lentulus gained his request from Caesar.

____

______ **13.** **Factā potestāte** (6) is ablative of description.

____

Name ______________________ Date __________ Period ____________

Activity 66h Vocabulary Skills: Sententia Scramble

Unscramble the clues, which are all mastery words appearing in Chapters 64, 65, and 66. Copy the letters in the numbered cells to the other cells with the same number to create a famous saying of Cicero.

Clue	Boxes (numbered cells)	Meaning
SLĒPB	5 boxes (3)	plebeians, common people
NIIVADI	7 boxes (2)	ill will, hatred, outrage
RASROT	6 boxes (11)	ships' beaks; speaker's platform
PEIMDĪTAEMN	11 boxes (10)	baggage
NAIMA	5 boxes (17)	soul; darling
SUTMUID	7 boxes (12)	eagerness, enthusiasm, support
SESPUROT	8 boxes (20)	next, following
NŌSUT	5 boxes (21)	known, well-known
SUTIULM	7 boxes (9)	last, least, farthest
CĀSUR	5 boxes (14)	dear, beloved
TIRNEIM	7 boxes (22)	meanwhile
PIĒRĪD	6 boxes (5)	on the day before
CICRĀ	5 boxes	around, about
VEHEER	6 boxes	to carry, convey
ROĪRĪ	5 boxes	to arise; begin
TALĒER	6 boxes (18)	to lie in hiding
SĒ REICERPE	2 boxes (1) + 8 boxes	to return, go back
SERNOTDEE	9 boxes	to show, point out
DUTSĒRE	7 boxes (4)	to be eager for, support
CEERIRE	7 boxes	to throw back, throw off
DĒLISĪRE	8 boxes (15)	to leap down
CIPNEERI	8 boxes (7)	to begin
IHROPBĒRE	9 boxes (13)	to prevent, prevent from (+ infin.)
PUEQERSĪ	8 boxes (8)	to follow, pursue
ĒNERĒCS	7 boxes (19)	to be of the opinion, think, advise, suggest
PRPEORĀRE	9 boxes (6)	to hurry
REMĒRĪ	6 boxes (16)	to deserve, earn

[1][2][3][ū][4]   [5][6][7][8][9][10]   [11][12][13][14][15][16][17]   [18][19][x]   [20][21][22]

"The safety of the people is the supreme law." (Cicero, *De legibus*)

Name ______________________ Date ________ Period __________

CHAPTER 67

An Exceptional Wife

Go Online PHSchool.com Web Code: jqd-0013

Activity 67a Reading Skills

Answer the following questions based on Reading 67A.

1. What figure of speech is found in line 1? ______________
   Copy out the Latin words that make up this figure:

   ____

   What is its effect?

   ____

2. This passage contains many nouns and adjectives that end in **-a**. Place a check mark in the appropriate blank to indicate whether each of these words is a noun, a substantive (adjective used in place of a noun), or an adjective; if an adjective, tell what it modifies.

   a. rāra (1) ____ noun ____ substantive ____ adj. modifying ______________

   b. diūturna (1) ____ noun ____ substantive ____ adj. modifying ______________

   c. mātrimōnia (1) ____ noun ____ substantive ____ adj. modifying ______________

   d. fīnīta (1) ____ noun ____ substantive ____ adj. modifying ______________

   e. interrupta (1) ____ noun ____ substantive ____ adj. modifying ______________

   f. vetusta (2) ____ noun ____ substantive ____ adj. modifying ______________

   g. domestica (3) ____ noun ____ substantive ____ adj. modifying ______________

   h. bona (3) ____ noun ____ substantive ____ adj. modifying ______________

   i. cētera (7) ____ noun ____ substantive ____ adj. modifying ______________

   j. innumerābilia (7) ____ noun ____ substantive ____ adj. modifying ______________

   k. commūnia (7) ____ noun ____ substantive ____ adj. modifying ______________

   l. propria (8) ____ noun ____ substantive ____ adj. modifying ______________

   m. tua (8) ____ noun ____ substantive ____ adj. modifying ______________

   n. similia (8) ____ noun ____ substantive ____ adj. modifying ______________

   o. tālia (9) ____ noun ____ substantive ____ adj. modifying ______________

Name ______________________ Date __________ Period __________

3. Using the grid below, analyze the last two sentences in Reading A (**Cūr dīcam . . . praestārent**). Number the clauses in the left-hand column.

		main clause (deliberative subjunctive)
		participial phrase 1

Activity 67b Reading Skills: Recognizing What You See

Answer the following questions, referring to B:5–7.

1. You know that a neuter noun such as **agmen** (5) can be either nominative or accusative. At what point does it become clear that **agmen** is the direct object?

____

2. What three participles modify **agmen**?

a. __________ **b.** __________ **c.** __________

In narrative Latin prose (i.e., when an author tells a story), events are normally presented in the order that they occur; explanations of how or why something happened usually come after the event they describe. The author uses a variety of structures (participles, ablative absolutes, subordinate clauses, as well as main verbs) to organize his ideas. Usually the main verb(s) express(es) the most important idea.

(continued)

Name ________________________________ Date __________ Period __________

3. Complete the following grid, providing a paraphrase (not a literal translation) to show what each event was.

	LATIN	ENGLISH
Event #1		a group of men was collected by Milo
Explanation of #1		
Event #2a & 2b	irruptūrum et dīreptūrum	
Event #3		
Event #4		

4. Are these events presented in chronological order? ______

5. Based on the principle stated in italics at the bottom of the previous page, what does the husband regard as the most important or main point of this sentence?

____

Activity 67c Writer's Techniques

1. Reading C begins with a deliberative subjunctive (**ēruam**, 1). Explain how this is also an example of a rhetorical question.

____

2. In what way is Reading C an extended example of preterition (see the Reading Note on page 175)?

____

____

3. What words (particularly verbs) in lines 2–5 of Reading C make it appear that the wife was mainly responsible for her husband's being saved?

____

____

____

____

Name ______________________ Date __________ Period __________

Activity 67d Language Skills: Syncopated Verbs

Review the Reading Note on page 179. Then fill in the blanks to show both the full form and the syncopated form of each verb.

	FULL FORM	SYNCOPATED FORM
1.	______________	ēvocāssent
2.	______________	ambulārit
3.	______________	dormīstī
4.	______________	cognōsse
5.	vindicāvissēmus	______________
6.	memorāverim	______________
7.	sepelīvistis	______________
8.	petīvisse	______________

Activity 67e Reading Skills: Structure of Narrative

*Most of Reading D consists of one long sentence (**Redditō mē . . . nōtēsceret**, 1–7). Analyze this sentence using the grid below. In the left column, write a phrase in English to summarize what took place in each part of the sentence. In the middle column, copy out the relevant Latin words (you may use ellipsis points). In the right column, indicate what structure the author uses to present each action. Some of the items are completed for you.*

WHAT HAPPENED	LATIN WORDS	STRUCTURE
husband was restored	*Redditō . . . patriae*	*ablative absolute*
explanation of how he was restored		
	cum per tē . . . interpellārētur	
		participial phrase
		*main verbs (with ellipsis of **es**)*
	livōribus . . . replēta	
wife reminded Lepidus about Octavian's decree		*ablative absolute*
	(cum) palam conquererēris	
		purpose clause

Name ______________________ Date __________ Period ____________

As stated in Activity 67b, narrative Latin prose usually presents events in the order that they occur, with the main verb(s) expressing the most important idea.

1. Are the events in this sentence presented in chronological order? ______

2. Based on what he chose as the main verbs in the sentence, what does the husband regard as the most important point that he is making? How does this agree with what he said in the first sentence of Reading D?

____

____

____

Activity 67f Writer's Techniques: The Husband's Feelings

Answer each question as directed, based on Reading D.

1. The words **in vītā mihi . . . tuā vice** (1) make a sort of chiasmus, where **mihi** contrasts with **tuā**. What is the effect of this chiastic phrase?

____

2. Copy out three Latin phrases that show how the wife was mistreated.

   a. ______________________________

   b. ______________________________

   c. ______________________________

3. Copy out three Latin phrases that express the husband's admiration for his wife's behavior.

   a. ______________________________

   b. ______________________________

   c. ______________________________

4. Copy out three Latin phrases that flatter Augustus.

   a. ______________________________

   b. ______________________________

   c. ______________________________

Name ______________________________ Date ________ Period __________

A ROMAN LOOKS AT CLEOPATRA

Activity 68a Reading Skills: Recognizing What You See

Copy out the Latin that corresponds to each English phrase, clause, or word group given below. Do not include any extra words.

1. Now we must drink ______________________________

2. with Salian feasts ______________________________

3. to decorate the couch ______________________________

4. while the queen was preparing ______________________________

5. mad ruin for the Capitol ______________________________

6. and destruction for the Empire ______________________________

7. with her polluted brood ______________________________

8. of foul men ______________________________

9. mad (enough) to hope for ______________________________

10. anything at all ______________________________

11. scarcely a single ship unharmed ______________________________

12. Caesar, pursuing closely with oars ______________________________

13. (her) as she flew from Italy ______________________________

14. like a hawk (pursues) soft doves ______________________________

15. to put in chains ______________________________

16. the destructive creature ______________________________

17. (she) did not dread the sword ______________________________

18. like a woman ______________________________

19. with tranquil expression ______

20. brave (enough) to handle ______

21. the scaly asps ______

22. to drink into her body ______

23. the dark poison ______

24. since her death was premeditated ______

25. refusing to be borne away ______

26. for a splendid triumphal procession ______

27. a not humble (proud) woman ______

Activity 68b Writer's Techniques: How the Cleopatra Ode Is Organized

It is possible to see this poem as divided into three separate units of thought. The punctuation helps you to determine in which stanzas the meaning carries over into the next one. Indicate the line numbers of each unit of thought in the spaces provided below and then summarize the content of each unit. Be sure to include a statement of how Horace feels about Cleopatra in each successive thought unit, citing relevant Latin words or phrases in support of your observations.

First Thought Unit

(Lines ______ to ______) ______

______

______

______

Second Thought Unit

(Lines ______ to ______) ______

______

______

______

Name ______________________ Date __________ Period __________

Third Thought Unit

(Lines ______ to ______) ______________________

____

____

____

____

Activity 68c Writer's Techniques: Poetic Imagery I

In his poems, Horace often uses imagery deriving from the wine culture created by the ancient Greeks and Romans. Find at least four examples of this imagery and explain its relevance to the context in which it is found. Write the pertinent Latin and the line numbers in which it is found.

1. ______________________

____

2. ______________________

____

3. ______________________

____

4. ______________________

____

5. ______________________

____

Name ______________________________ Date __________ Period ____________

Activity 68d Writer's Techniques: Poetic Imagery II

Review the description of the figure of speech metonymy on page 185. For each example of metonymy underlined in this activity, give the correct form of the more common object which is provided in parentheses. Then explain the relationship between the substitution and the more common object. These examples are selected from Latin poetry.

1. **Arma virumque canō.** ____________________ **(bellum)**

   I sing of arms and a man. (*Aeneid* 1.1)

   ____

2. **Implentur veteris Bacchī pinguisque ferīnae.** ____________________ **(vīnum)**

   (Aeneas' men) are filled with old Bacchus and fat game. (*Aeneid* 1.215)

   ____

3. **Tum omnibus ūna omnēs surripuit Venerēs.** ____________________ **(pulchritūdō, -inis)**

   Then (Lesbia) alone has stolen away all the charms from all (other women). (Catullus 86.6)

   ____

4. **Fūnus et imperiō parābat.** ____________________ **(mors, mortis)**

   (Cleopatra) was preparing a funeral for the empire. (Horace, *Odes* 1.37.8; cf. 68:8)

   ____

5. **Frustrā cruentō Marte carēbimus.** ____________________ **(bellum)**

   In vain we will lack bloody Mars. (Horace, *Odes* 2.14.13)

   ____

6. **Velut crīmen taedās exōsa iugālēs. . . .** ____________________ **(nūptiae)**

   (Daphne) hating the wedding torches as an evil thing. (Ovid, *Metamorphoses* 1.483)

   ____

7. **Labōre fessī vēnimus lārem ad nostrum.** ____________________ **(domus)**

   Weary of the labor (of travel), we came to our household god. (Catullus, Poem 31.9)

   ____

Why do you think Roman poets such as Horace use this figure of speech? What do they gain from such substitutions?

____

Name ______________________________ Date __________ Period __________

Activity 68e Writer's Techniques: Two Views of Actium

*Lines 12–16 of this poem allude to a significant historical event involving both Octavian (**Caesar**, 16) and Cleopatra. Return to Reading 56B:9–13 to review the details of this event and then answer the following questions in English.*

1. Who is the unexpressed subject of **dum cupiditāte muliebrī optat etiam in urbe rēgnāre**? (10) How is this person characterized here?

____

2. What does the ablative absolute **cōgente uxōre Cleopatrā** (9) further suggest about this individual, in the opinion of the writer Eutropius?

____

3. Translate 56C:10–12 to review what happened to this individual.

____

____

____

Now return to the reading in Chapter 68 to answer the following.

4. a. How is the battle of Actium described in the Cleopatra ode (13)?

____

____

b. What two effects did Caesar's victory have on the queen?

____

____

5. Why do you suppose Horace omitted any mention of Antony in the Cleopatra ode?

____

____

Name ______________________________ Date __________ Period ____________

Activity 68f Sight Reading

Augustus and the deaths of Antony and Cleopatra.

Aegyptum petit obsessāque Alexandrīā, quō Antōnius cum Cleopatrā cōnfūgerat, brevī potītus est. Et Antōnium quidem, sērās condiciōnēs pācis temptantem, ad mortem adēgit vīditque mortuum. Cleopatrae, quam servātam triumphō magnopere cupiēbat, etiam Psyllōs admōvit, quī venēnum ac vīrus exūgerent, quod perisse morsū aspidis putābātur. Ambōbus commūnem sepultūrae honōrem tribuit ac tumulum ab ipsīs incohātum perficī iussit. Reliquōs Antōniī rēgīnaeque commūnēs līberōs nōn secus ac necessitūdine iūnctōs sibi et cōnservāvit et mox prō condiciōne cuiusque sustinuit ac fōvit.

—Suetonius, *Vita Augusti*

1 **petit**: the subject is Augustus
2 **brevī**: = **brevī tempore**
sērus, -a, um, *too late, final*
3 **Cleopatrae**: dative with **admōvit** (4)
servātam: = **servātam esse**
triumphō: dative
4 **Psyllī**: a people of Africa celebrated for drawing out snake venom from a bite
vīrus, -ī, n., *poison*; note the gender
exūgō, exūgere, exūgī, *to drain away, draw out*
morsus, -ūs, m., *bite*
aspis, aspidis, f., *asp, poisonous snake*
5 **ambōbus**: dative plural of **ambō**
commūnem: agrees with **honōrem**, but take with **sepultūrae**
tumulus, -ī, m., *tomb*
6 **incohātus, -a, -um**, *begun* (but not finished)
nōn secus, *not otherwise, no differently*
7 **ac necessitūdine iunctōs sibi**: *than if joined to him by close relationship*, i.e. his own family
prō condiciōne cuiusque: *in a manner suitable to the rank of each*
8 **foveō, fovēre, fōvī, fōtus**, *to cherish, support*

1. What did Augustus do after reaching Egypt? (1–2)

____

2. What was Antony attempting to do before he died? (2)

____

3. What is the meaning of the phrase **(Augustus) ad mortem adēgit**? (2–3)

____

4. What does **vīdit mortuum** (3) indicate that Augustus did? Why do you think he did this?

____

Name ______________________ Date __________ Period __________

5. Why did Augustus summon the Psylli, even though the queen was already dead? (4–5)

____

6. For what reason did he greatly desire Cleopatra to live? (3)

____

7. In what two ways did Augustus honor Antony and Cleopatra after they died? (5–6)

a. ____

b. ____

8. What happened to the children of Antony and Cleopatra? (6–8)

____

____

Name ________________________ Date ________ Period ____________

CHAPTER 69

Augustus

Activity 69a Reading Skills: Recognizing What You See

Using the grid below, divide the text of Reading A into sense units in the left-hand column that correspond with the grammatical function of each sense unit given in the right-hand column. Be sure to indent where appropriate, as you have done in previous such activities.

	participial phrase
	main clause
	relative clause begins
	participial phrase
	relative clause ends
	main clause begins
	ablative absolute
	participial phrase
	main clause ends
	indirect command clause
	main clause
	main clause begins
	cum causal clause
	main clause ends
	relative clause
	main clause begins
	participial phrase 1
	main clause continues
	participial phrase 2
	main clause ends

Name ______________________ Date __________ Period ____________

Activity 69b Writer's Techniques: Imperial Propaganda I

1. Return to Eutropius' *Breviarium* in Chapters 55D:9–17 and 56A:8–14. The passages from Eutropius and the portions of the *Res gestae* of Augustus in this chapter are summaries of the events of the years immediately following the assassination of Julius Caesar. After rereading Eutropius and the passage written by Augustus in Reading A, answer the following question: What is the focus of Augustus' writing, as opposed to that of Eutropius? What do the emperor's own words tell you about him?

____

____

____

____

____

____

____

2. Look at the pictures of the inscribed portion of the *Res gestae* on page 193 of the textbook and the temple wall on which it was inscribed on page 195. What conclusions can you draw about Augustus from this monument and from the content of its inscription?

____

____

____

____

____

____

____

____

Name ______________________ Date __________ Period __________

Activity 69c Language Skills: Indirect Statement

Summarize the content of that portion of the Res gestae *given in Reading D by composing in Latin the following sentences, all of which contain indirect statements. Use the vocabulary in Reading D for reference.*

1. The emperor wrote that he had restored Pompey's theater without any inscription of his name (on it).

   ____

2. Augustus writes that he repaired the aqueduct channels that were collapsing from old age.

   ____

3. Most Romans knew that many works begun by his father had been completed by Augustus.

   ____

4. Augustus says that he will order the basilica, having been destroyed by fire, to be completed by his heirs.

   ____

5. The emperor believed that many temples ought to be restored.

   ____

Activity 69d Writer's Techniques: Imperial Propaganda II

Augustus is thought by most modern historians to have usurped the powers once held by the Senate and the various magistrates of the Roman Republic. What does Augustus himself have to say about this? Translate the following two sentences from Reading B as your answer to this question.

Lines 1–3: In cōnsulātū sextō et septimō, postquam bella cīvīlia exstīnxeram, per cōnsēnsum ūniversōrum potītus rērum omnium, rem pūblicam ex meā potestāte in senātūs populīque Rōmānī arbitrium trānstulī.

____

____

____

Lines 7–9: Post id tempus auctōritāte omnibus praestitī, potestātis autem nihil amplius habuī quam cēterī quī mihi quoque in magistrātū collēgae fuērunt.

____

____

Name ______________________ Date __________ Period ____________

Activity 69e Language Skills: Review of *Cum* Clauses

Review the various types of ***cum*** *clauses found on page 201 in the textbook. Then identify the* ***cum*** *clause in each of the following sentences as A. circumstantial, B. causal, C. temporal, or D. concessive (although). Which one of these is not found with a subjunctive verb? Write the letter of the correct identification in the space provided, and then translate the entire sentence. Remember to use the context of the sentence in determining the most appropriate meaning of* ***cum****.*

1. Pāx, cum portae Iānī Quirīnī clausae sunt, tōtō in orbe terrārum est. ______

____

2. Augustus, cum cōnsul nōn semper esset, tamen potestātem tribūnī habēbat. ______

____

____

3. Octāviānus, cum bella cīvīlia exstīnxisset, senātūs cōnsultō Augustus appellātus est. ______

____

____

4. Cum Augustus ex Hispāniā Galliāque redierat, tum multī senātōrēs eum salūtābant. ______

____

____

5. Octāviānus, cum Caesar ā factiōne senatōrum occīsus esset, illōs senatōrēs in exsilium expulsōs in proeliō bis vīcit. ______

____

____

6. Multa opera, cum ab Augustō incohāta essent, hērēdibus eius perficienda erant. ______
(**incohō, āre, -āvī, -atus,** *to undertake, begin*)

____

____

7. Cum Augustus annōs LXXVI nātus mortuus est, Tiberius imperātor factus est. ______

____

____

Name ______________________ Date __________ Period __________

Activity 69f Sight Readings

Answer the questions on the following lines from the Aeneid, *in which Vergil describes the gates of war (C:9 in the textbook) in a poetic manner. In this passage Jupiter is foretelling how Augustus Caesar will bring peace to the Roman world. The words* **Fīdēs**, **Bellī**, *and* **Furor** *are capitalized because they each personify an abstract idea.*

Reading I

Aspera tum positīs mītēscunt saecula bellīs;
cāna Fīdēs et Vesta, Remō cum frātre Quirīnus
iūra dabunt; dīrae ferrō et compāgibus artīs
claudentur Bellī portae; Furor impius intus
saeva sedēns super arma et centum vīnctus aēnīs
post tergum nōdīs fremet horridus ōre cruentō.

1 **asper, aspera, asperum,** *harsh, fierce*
positīs: = **dēpositīs**
mītēscō, mītēscere, *to become mild, calm*
saeculum, -ī, n., *age*
2 **cānus, -a, -um,** *white; grizzled, gray*
Quirīnus, -ī, m., Romulus
3 **iūs, iūris,** n., *justice, law, right*
dīrus, -a, -um, *terrible, awful*
compāgēs, compāgis, f., *joint, fastening*
artus, -a, -um, *close-fitting*
4 **intus,** adv., *within, inside*
5 **saevus, -a, -um,** *savage, cruel*
vinciō, vincīre, vinxī, vīnctus, *to bind, tie up*
aēnus, -a, -um, *(of) bronze*
6 **post tergum:** *behind his back*
nōdus, ī, m., *knot*
fremō, fremere, fremuī, fremitus, *to rage, roar*
cruentus, -a, -um, *cruel, bloody*

1. What introductory comment does the poet make about the times he is describing? (1)

____

2. What type of word order do you notice in line 1? Cite the Latin words.

____

3. What grammatical construction is **positīs . . . bellīs** (1)? Translate it.

____

4. Who or what is responsible for bringing law to Rome? (2–3)

____

5. How are the **Bellī portae** described? (3–4)

____

6. What is kept inside the gates? Cite the relevant Latin phrase. (4)

____

Name ______________________ Date __________ Period ____________

7. Describe this personification as portrayed in lines 5–6.

____

____

8. What form is **vīnctus** (5) and what does it modify?

____

9. To whom and to what is Vergil alluding in this passage?

____

____

10. Locate and write out six Latin words or phrases that help set the tone of this passage.

a. ____________________ **d.** ____________________

b. ____________________ **e.** ____________________

c. ____________________ **f.** ____________________

Reading II

Vergil also describes the shrine or gateway of Janus later in the Aeneid. *On separate paper, write a short essay in which you compare and contrast this description with the one given above. In what ways are the descriptions the same? In what ways are they different? Cite relevant words and phrases from the Latin texts of both in support of your answer.*

Sunt geminae Bellī portae (sīc nōmine dīcunt)
rēligiōne sacrae et saevī formīdine Martis;
centum aereī claudunt vectēs aeternaque ferrī
rōbora, nec custōs absistit līmine Iānus.

1 **geminus, -a, -um,** *double, twin*
2 **rēligiōne**: *religious awe;* ablative of cause or means
sacrae: supply a word such as **factae**
formīdō, formīdinis, f., *terror, dread*
3 **aereus, -a, -um,** *brazen, bronze*
vectis, vectis, f., *bar, bolt*
ferrum, -ī, n., *iron*
4 **rōbor, rōboris,** n., *oak; strength*
absistō, absistere, abstitī, *to go away, leave*

Name ______________________ Date ________ Period ____________

AN EMPEROR'S DAUGHTER

CHAPTER 70

Activity 70a Reading Skills: Truth and Fiction

Answer the following questions about Reading A, lines 1–4.

1. Go to the picture of the coin on page 203 of the textbook and write its Latin legend in the space provided below (expand the abbreviations).

____

2. Go to Reading A, lines 3–4, and compare Suetonius' account with the information given in the legend.

____

____

____

3. How were consuls chosen during the time of the Republic? How do the sources given above provide evidence that Augustus had not restored the Republic to its former status? (Cf. 69B: 2–3 and 7–9.)

____

____

Activity 70b Language Skills: Forms and Uses

Answer the following questions about Reading A, lines 5–8.

1. Write the introductory word that introduces the first result clause and the subjunctive verbs that complete it. introductory word ______________;
   subjunctive verb 1 ______________; subjunctive verb 2 ______________

2. Do the same for the second result clause:
   introductory word ______________; subjunctive verb ______________

3. Who or what is the unstated subject of **assuefaceret** and **vetāret** (5)? ______________

4. Circle the verb that would correctly complete the conditional clause **nisi propalam** (6):
   a. est b. esset c. erat d. fuisset

Name ______________________ Date __________ Period ____________

5. Identify the boundaries of the relative clause of characteristic that you find in these lines.

_______________ and _______________

6. Basing your answer on its context, explain why **coetū** (7) is an ablative of separation.

____

7. The infinitive **fēcisse** is translated in line 8 as:

a. has behaved   b. was behaving   c. is behaving   d. had behaved

8. True or False? Circle whether the following is true or false; then correct it if it is false. The verb **vēnisset** is subjunctive because it is found in a relative clause of characteristic.

____

Activity 70c Writer's Techniques: Supporting Details

The imperial biographer Suetonius likes to give examples in support of generalized statements that he makes. Answer the following questions about Reading B.

1. What is the general statement about Augustus that Suetonius makes in line 1?

____

2. What Latin phrase summarizes the point of this sentence? _______________

3. Giving consideration to word selection and position, identify two ways in which Suetonius emphasizes this point.

   a. ____

   b. ____

4. Write the Latin that expresses the first example of why Suetonius says **fortūna dēseruit.**

____

5. Write the Latin that expresses the second example of why Suetonius says **fortūna dēseruit.**

____

6. What does the sentence in line 4 tell us about Augustus' relative feelings about these two events?

____

(continued)

Name ____________________ Date __________ Period __________

7. Suetonius goes on to explain how Augustus reacted to this disgrace (4–6), further exemplifying the point he made in his opening sentence. Write the specific Latin that corresponds with the English.

   a. For he (his spirit) was not so much broken

   ____

   b. by the loss of Gaius and Lucius

   ____

   c. (but) he informed the Senate about his daughter

   ____

   d. without being present

   ____

   e. and through a letter read aloud by the quaestor

   ____

   f. and he refrained from the company of people for a long time

   ____

   g. because of his shame

   ____

   h. he even thought about executing (Julia).

   ____

Activity 70d Language Skills: Review

Locate in Reading C an example in Latin of each of the following forms and match it with its example.

______	present participle	**a.** relēgātae (9)
______	present passive infinitive	**b.** fieret (10)
______	complementary infinitive	**c.** esset (11)
______	subjunctive verb in indirect command	**d.** alī (16)
______	subjunctive verb in a result clause	**e.** continērētur (19)
______	past participle used as a substantive	**f.** ingemēscēns (19)
______	subjunctive verb in an indirect question	**g.** prōclāmāre (19)

Name ______________________________ Date __________ Period ____________

There are four comparative adjectives and one comparative adverb in this reading. Find and cite them below.

Adjectives

________________ ________________ ________________ ________________

Adverb

____

Activity 70e Short Essay: Three Roman Women

In Book III you have met three women from Roman antiquity: the unnamed wife in Chapter 67 and now Julia Maior and Julia Minor, daughter and granddaughter of Augustus. On separate paper, summarize what made the wife in Chapter 67 such a model of Roman womanhood. How do the two Julias compare to her? Support your observations by citing and translating relevant words or phrases from the Latin texts.

Activity 70f Language Skills: The Supine

Review the Reading Note on page 207. Then underline the past participle or supine in each of the following sentences. Indicate whether the underlined form is a past participle or a supine by circling the appropriate designation. Then translate the sentence.

1. Imperātor, cum nepōtēs cōnsulēs dēsignātī erant, senātōrēs quōsdam mīsit eōs salūtātum. Participle Supine

____

2. Cūr Vinicius Iūliam vīsitātum Baiās vēnit? Participle Supine

____

3. Suētōnius scrīpsit Augustum fīliam suam necāre velle, horribile audītū. Participle Supine

____

4. Augustus nepōtem Agrippam, senātūs cōnsultō condemnātum, ad īnsulam trānsportāvit. Participle Supine

____

5. Populus Rōmānus dēprecābātur ut imperātor Agrippam ad īnsulam missum revocāret. (**dēprecor, -ārī, -ātus sum**, *to entreat, plead*) Participle Supine

____

6. Volēbatne imperātor fīliam suam necāre, mīrābile dictū? Participle Supine

____

Name ______________________ Date __________ Period __________

Activity 70g Language Skills: Subordinate Clauses Inside an Indirect Statement

Part A

Review the Reading Note on page 207. Then select the verb form that best completes each sentence and write it in the space provided. Use the context to help you determine the correct form. Then translate the sentence.

1. Augustus senātōribus dīcēbat sē fīliam suam in exsilium mittere, quod plūrima scelesta ______________. (fēcisse, facienda, facta sunt, fēcisset)

____

____

2. Suētōnius scīvit sibi ubi Lūcius Caesar ______________ cognōscendum esse. (mortuus esset, moriētur, moritūrum esse, mortuus est)

____

____

3. Suētōnius scrībit nēminem cūr Phoebē suspendiō vītam ______________ cognōscere. (fīnīverit, fīniēbat, fīnīta erat, fīnīta esset)

____

____

4. Augustus dīxit Iūliae vīnum bibere nōn licēre cum in exsilium ______________. (mīsisse, missa esset, mīsisset, missum est)

____

____

5. Multī putāvērunt Augustum ut ipse exemplum ______________ fīliam neptemque in exsilium mīsisse. (**neptis, neptis,** f., *granddaughter*) (praebēre, praebuisse, praebēbat, praebēret)

____

____

Part B

Review the information on nested clauses given on pages 35 and 87 of the textbook. Then, in three of the sentences in Part A, double underline the entire subordinate clause that is nested within the indirect statement.

Name ______________________ Date __________ Period ____________

Activity 70h Sight Reading

Scribonia and Livia

Mox Scrībōniam in mātrimonium accēpit nūptam ante duōbus cōnsulāribus, ex alterō etiam mātrem. Cum hāc quoque dīvortium fēcit, "pertaesus," ut scrībit, "mōrum perversitātem eius," ac statim Līviam Drūsīllam mātrimoniō Tiberī Nerōnis et quidem praegnantem abdūxit dīlēxitque et prōbāvit ūnicē ac persevēranter. Ex Scrībōniā Iūliam, ex Līvia nihil līberōrum tulit, cum maximē cuperet. Īnfāns, quī conceptus erat, immātūrus est ēditus.

—Suetonius, *Vita Augusti* (extracts)

1 **accēpit**: the unexpressed subject is Augustus
nūbō, nūbere, nūpsī, nūptūrus + dat., *to cover with a veil; to marry*

2 **mātrem**: in apposition to **Scrībōniam** (1)
hāc: Scrībōnia
pertaedet, pertaedēre, pertaesus est, *to cause weariness*
pertaesus: supply **sum**
mōs, mōris, m., *custom, habit*; pl., *conduct, behavior*

3 **perversitās, perversitātis**, f., *irritability, obstinacy*
Tiberī Nerōnis: (wife of) Tiberius Nero

4 **prōbō, -āre, -āvī -ātus**, *to approve of; esteem, respect*
ūnicē, adv., *especially, particularly*
persevēranter, adv., *persistently, continually*

6 **immātūrus est ēditus**: *was born prematurely*

Answer the following questions in English.

1. What do we learn about Scribonia from the sentence in lines 1–2?

____

2. What reason does Augustus give for divorcing her? (2–3)

____

3. Whom does Augustus marry next? (3)

____

4. What do we learn about this woman? (3–4)

____

(continued)

Name ______________________ Date __________ Period __________

5. How are Augustus' feelings toward this woman described in line 4?

____

6. Who was Julia's mother? (4–5) _______________________

7. What do we learn about Livia's children? (5) _______________________

8. What is the understood subject of **cuperet** (5)? What does the clause **cum maximē cuperet** tell us about this person?

____

9. What sad event occurred to this person's only child? (5–6)

____

Name ______________________ Date ________ Period __________

CHAPTER 71

POET AND PRINCEPS

Activity 71a Meter: Elegiac Couplet

Mark the scansion of the following lines and practice reading them aloud. See pages 308–309 in the textbook for general help with meter; the meter of this poem is elegiac couplet, page 311.

Stulte, quid haec frūstrā vōtīs puerīlibus optās,
    quae nōn ūlla tibī fertque feretque diēs?
Sī semel optandum est, Augustī nūmen adōrā,
    et, quem sēnsistī, rīte precāre deum.
Ille tibī pennāsque potest currūsque volucrēs
    trādere. Det reditum, prōtinus āles eris.
Sī precer hoc (neque enim possum maiōra rogāre) [ma- is a long syllable]
    nē mea sint, timeō, vōta modesta parum.
Forsitan hoc ōlim, cum iam satiāverit īram,
    tum quoque sollicitā mente rogandus erit.
Quod minus intereā est, īnstar mihi mūneris amplī,
    ex hīs mē iubeat quōlibet īre locīs.

Activity 71b Writer's Techniques: Request to an Emperor

Review the section in the textbook on Reading Latin Poetry, page 119, and the Reading Note on parallel structure, page 153. Then answer the following questions about Reading 71A.

1. What figure of speech appears in lines 1, 3, and 5? ____________________

What is the effect of this figure?

____

2. In what ways are lines 1, 3, and 5 a sophisticated example of parallel structure?

____

____

Name ______________________________ Date __________ Period __________

3. How do lines 2, 4, and 6 follow the principle about elegiac couplets stated on page 119 of the textbook?

____

____

4. In lines 13–16 Ovid speaks of Augustus as if he were a god. Cite two Latin nouns and two verbs that make this explicit.

noun 1 ____________________ verb 1 ____________________

noun 2 ____________________ verb 2 ____________________

5. The Romans believed that a religious ceremony had to be performed perfectly in order to achieve its objective of obtaining the good will of the gods. What Latin word in lines 11–15 reflects this idea? Write this word and its English meaning.

____________________, meaning ____________________

6. How does Ovid bring back items from the first ten lines of the poem in order to stress the power of Augustus?

____

____

____

7. Ovid's great mythological poem, the *Metamorphoses*, is full of stories about gods who become angry and punish humans. How do lines 17–20 reflect a desire to avoid angering the godlike Augustus?

____

____

____

8. How does Ovid's actual request (lines 21–22) build upon the ideas expressed in the previous ten lines?

____

____

____

____

____

____

Name ______________________ Date __________ Period __________

Activity 71c Reading Skills: Modifiers of Nouns

1. In Reading A below, draw an arrow from each underlined modifier (adjective, participle, or noun in the genitive) to the noun or pronoun it modifies. Some arrows will point forward, others backward. If necessary, check genders of nouns in the textbook. The first one is completed for you.

Nunc ego Triptolemī cuperem cōnsistere currū,
mīsit in ignōtam quī rude sēmen humum;
nunc ego Mēdēae vellem frēnāre dracōnēs,
quōs habuit fugiēns arce, Corinthe, tuā;
nunc ego iactandās optārem sūmere pennās,
sīve tuās, Perseu, Daedale, sīve tuās:
ut tenerā nostrīs cēdente volātibus aurā
aspicerem patriae dulce repente solum,
dēsertaeque domūs vultūs, memorēsque sodālēs,
cāraque praecipuē coniugis ōra meae.
Stulte, quid haec frūstrā vōtīs puerīlibus optās,
quae nōn ūlla tibī fertque feretque diēs?
Sī semel optandum est, Augustī nūmen adōrā,
et, quem sēnsistī, rīte precāre deum.
Ille tibī pennāsque potest currūsque volucrēs
trādere. Det reditum, prōtinus āles eris.
Sī precer hoc (neque enim possum maiōra rogāre)
nē mea sint, timeō, vōta modesta parum.
Forsitan hoc ōlim, cum iam satiāverit īram,
tum quoque sollicitā mente rogandus erit.
Quod minus intereā est, īnstar mihi mūneris amplī,
ex hīs mē iubeat quōlibet īre locīs.

2. How many modifiers appear in front of their nouns? ______

3. How many appear after? ______

4. Do modifiers of nouns most often come before or after in Latin prose? ______________
Placement of modifiers of nouns is one significant difference between Latin prose and poetry.

Activity 71d Reading Skills: Outside the Boundaries

You know how important it is to observe boundaries of subordinate clauses. Usually each clause begins with a clear marker, either a relative pronoun or a conjunction. Sometimes, however, elements that belong inside a clause spill over to the left, i.e., appear in front of the clause marker. Also, sometimes a relative pronoun appears before its antecedent, not after it. Rewrite each of the following segments so that the words come in more common order.

1. mīsit in ignōtam quī rude sēmen humum (line 2)

____

2. et, quem sēnsistī, rīte precāre deum (line 14)

____

3. quīque per autumnum percussīs frīgore prīmō est color in foliīs (lines 29–30)

____

4. Nec melius valeō, quam corpore, mente (line 33)

____

5. tantus amor necis est, querar ut cum Caesaris īrā (line 39)

____

Activity 71e Language Skills: Future Passive Participle

Review the Reading Note on page 217. Then circle the future passive participle in each sentence, draw an arrow to the noun it modifies, underline the participial phrase, and translate the entire sentence. (Two of the sentences have no phrase to underline.)

1. Poēta dē librīs proximō annō scrībendīs cōgitat.

____

Name ______________________ Date __________ Period __________

2. Magister librōs in capsam pōnendās tenēbat. **capsa, -ae**, f., *storage case* (for scrolls)

____

3. Prīnceps nōmen poētae in exsilium mittendī mīlitibus dedit.

____

4. Prīnceps scelestōs pūniendōs in exsilium mittet.

____

5. Grammaticus aliquōs versūs Ovidiī hodiē legendōs trādidit.

____

6. Ovidius dē Augustī nūmine adōrandō scrīpsit.

____

Activity 71f Questions for Thought and Discussion

Answer the following questions on separate paper.

1. You have already analyzed how Ovid speaks of Augustus as a god. Is this just flattery of the emperor or does it reflect something more fundamental about what was happening in the Roman empire during the reign of Augustus?

2. The poem can be divided into four sections: lines 1–10, 11–22, 23–34, and 35–42. What is the main idea of each section? How do the sections relate to the main idea of the poem?

3. In what ways does Ovid convey his deep unhappiness at being forced to live in Tomis? Cite the Latin for specific images. Does this poem make you sympathize with Ovid? Why or why not?

4. How do you react when Ovid complains that Augustus should have executed him (lines 39–40)? Why do you think Ovid put this idea in the poem?

5. Do you think that a poem like this might have moved Augustus to change the conditions of Ovid's exile? Why or why not?

6. You have seen how Augustus banished both members of his own family and others whose actions displeased him. Does such banishment seem like a fair or appropriate practice? Why or why not? Did Augustus have any alternatives available to him?

Name ________________________________ Date ________ Period ___________

CHAPTER 72

DIDO AND AENEAS

Activity 72a Writer's Techniques: Rhetorical Questions

Review rhetorical questions in the Reading Note on page 69. Then outline each point Dido makes in her speech to Aeneas in Reading A by paraphrasing the content of each question in the spaces provided below.

1. **Dissimulāre . . . terra?** (305–306)

   ____

2. **Nec . . . Dīdō?** (307–308)

   ____

3. **Quīn . . . crūdēlis?** (309–311)

   ____

4. **Quid . . . aequor?** (311–313)

   ____

5. **Mēne fugis?** (314)

   ____

6. **Cui . . . restat?** (323–324)

   ____

7. **Quid moror?** (325)

   ____

8. **An . . . Iarbās?** (325–326)

   ____

Name ______________________ Date __________ Period ____________

Activity 72b Writer's Techniques: Drawing Attention or Creating Emphasis

Identify by name and describe how the following devices in Reading A emphasize the poet's meaning in each case. If necessary, go back to the appropriate Reading Note to review the figure of speech.

1. **Nec . . . nec . . . nec** (307–308) (Review the Reading Note on page 71.)

   ____

2. **Nec tē noster amor**
   nec tē data dextera quondam
   nec moritūra tenet crūdēlī fūnere Dīdō? (307–308) (See the Reading Note on page 221.)

   ____

3. **hībernō sīdere** (309) (See the Reading Note on page 20.)

   ____

4. **Mēne fugis?** (314). (Comment on the position of **Mē**.)

   ____

5. **Per ego hās lacrimās dextramque tuam tē, . . . per cōnūbia nostra, per inceptōs hymenaeōs** (314–316) (Review the Reading Note on page 71.)

   ____

6. **Tē propter . . . tē propter** (320–321)

   ____

   Note: The object of a preposition sometimes precedes the preposition. Given this example, can you think of a reason why?

   ____

Name ______________________ Date __________ Period __________

Activity 72c Reading Skills: Prepositions Omitted with Compound Verbs

In the Reading Note on page 220, you learned that the ablative case is often used without a preposition if the prefix of a compound verb expresses the necessary idea. Circle the prefix, draw an arrow from the prefix to the ablative case word, and translate the sentence.

1. Imber caelō in nāvēs Troiānās effundēbātur.

   Rain poured out from the sky onto the Trojan ships.

2. Dīdō adiūvit Troiānōs nāvibus ēiectōs tempestāte.

   ____

3. Rēgīna turre dēcucurrit ut Aenēān urbe ēnāvigantem vidēret.

   ____

4. Cognōscēbatne Aenēās īram pectore Dīdōnis inclūsam esse?

   ____

5. Tantae lāmentātiōnēs gemitūsque ātriō efferēbantur ut ad caelum pervenīrent.

   ____

Activity 72d Meter: Dactylic Hexameter

Scan the following lines from Reading B and then read them aloud. Pay close attention to the places where elision may occur. See pages 309 and 311 in the textbook for help if needed. Then answer the questions below.

Mē patris Anchīsae, quotiēns ūmentibus umbrīs
nox operit terrās, quotiēns astra ignea surgunt,
admonet in somnīs et turbida terret imāgō;
mē puer Ascanius capitisque iniūria cārī,
quem rēgnō Hesperiae fraudō et fātālibus arvīs.
Nunc etiam interpres dīvum Iove missus ab ipsō
(testor utrumque caput) celerēs mandāta per aurās
dētulit: ipse deum manifestō in lūmine vīdī
intrantem mūrōs vōcemque hīs auribus hausī.
Dēsine mēque tuīs incendere tēque querēlīs;
Ītaliam nōn sponte sequor."

Name ______________________ Date __________ Period __________

1. How many elisions can you find in the passage? ______

____

2. How many dactyls are there in line 356? ______

How many spondees in line 357? ______

3. Does the frequency of dactyls in the second half of lines 356 and 357 suggest movement that is fast or slow? Consider the context.

____

4. What consonantal sound seems to dominate lines 358–359? Is the mood of these lines lively and spirited? Serious and solemn? Sad and morose?

____

5. The alternation of long and short syllables is often used to suggest high emotion. Explain why the poet uses this rhythm in lines 360–361. What is Aeneas' emotional state here? Support your answer from the Latin text.

____

Activity 72e Reading Skills: Details of Dido's Death

Answer the following analysis questions about lines 651–662 of Reading D.

1. To whom or what is Dido speaking these words?

____

Note: Direct address to an absent object or person is a figure of speech known as *apostrophe.*

2. What figure of speech do you see in line 652? (Hint: consider word order)

____

3. What type of ablative is **hīs . . . cūrīs** (652)? How do you know?

____

4. Write out in more usual word order the relative clause in line 653. Why is the word order here unusual?

____

____

(continued)

5. Explain why the subjunctive mood (**tetigissent**) is used in the conditional clause **sī . . . carīnae** (657–658). (Review pages 96–97.)

______

6. What or whom does the adjective **fēlīx** (657) modify?

______

7. The noun **carīnae** (658) means keel of a ship. For what more prosaic meaning is it substituted here? What figure of speech is this and why is it used?

______

8. Explain the difference in mood and tense between **moriēmur** (659) and **moriāmur** (660).

______

9. What adjective modifies **Dardanus**? (662) ______

10. What does Dido mean by what she says in lines 661–662?

______

Activity 72f Language Skills: Verb Forms

In each of the following, there is a verb that is spelled in an unusual manner, i.e., there is a syllable or a form of the word **esse** *missing, or there is another variation in the way the verb is spelled. Review the Reading Notes on pages 89, 179, and 222 if needed. Circle the less common verb form in each sentence and then give the more usual spelling.*

1. Dissimulāre etiam spērāstī, perfide, tantum posse nefās (305) ______

2. Tē propter Libycae gentēs Nomadumque tyrannī ōdēre (320–321) ______

3. Tē propter eundem exstīnctus pudor (321–322) ______

4. Ego tē, quae plūrima fandō ēnumerāre valēs, numquam, rēgīna, negābō prōmeritam (333–334) ______

5. Sed nunc . . . Ītaliam Lyciae iussēre capessere sortēs (345–346) ______

6. Hyrcānae admōrunt ūbera tigrēs (367) ______

7. Nusquam tūta fidēs______. (373) (Hint: what is needed to complete this sentence?)

______

8. Spērō equidem mediīs . . . supplicia hausūrum______ scopulīs et nōmine Dīdō saepe vocatūrum ______. (382–384) (Hint: what are needed to complete these verb forms?)

______

9. (Anna) audiit exanimis . . . per mediōs ruit (672–674) ______

10. Eadem mē ad fāta vocāssēs. (678) ______

11. Exstīnxtī tē mēque, soror, populumque patrēsque Sīdoniōs urbemque tuam. (682–683)

______

12. Conticuēre omnēs intentīque ōra tenēbant (II.1) ______

Activity 72g Language Skills: Expressing Purpose

You have now met four ways to express purpose in Latin. Review the consolidation of expressions of purpose on page 240. Underline the expression of purpose in each of the following sentences and then translate the entire sentence.

1. Aenēās ad Hesperiam nāvigābat Troiae novae condendae causā.

______

2. Pater omnipotēns nūntium suum dēmīsit quī Aenēan admonēret.

______

3. Amābatne Dīdō Troiānum urbis suae tuendae grātiā? (**tueor, tuērī, tuitus sum,** *to keep safe, protect*)

______

4. Rēgīna gladium Aenēae quō sē occīdat habet.

______

5. Clāmōribus auditīs, fēminae ad rēgiam cucurrērunt quid factum esset cognitum.

______

6. Fāma ad rem omnibus nūntiāndam concussam per urbem bacchātur. (**bacchor, bacchārī, bacchātus sum,** *to rave, run riot*)

______

(continued)

Name ____________________ Date __________ Period __________

7. Īris Olympō dēmissa est crīnem rēgīnae morientis sectum.
(**secō, secāre, secuī, sectus**, *to cut, snip*)

____

8. Dēscendetne ad īnferōs pius Aenēās ad Dīdōnem videndam?

____

9. Īnfēlīx Dīdō Annam sorōrem relīquit quae urbem Carthāginem regeret.

____

Activity 72h Sight Reading

In the following passage, Dido again brings down a series of curses on Aeneas and the Trojans. In these curses, Dido alludes to Hannibal and the Punic Wars.

"Tum vōs, ō Tyriī, stirpem et genus omne futūrum
exercēte odiīs, cinerīque haec mittite nostrō
mūnera. Nūllus amor populīs nec foedera suntō.
Exoriāre aliquis nostrīs ex ossibus ultor,
quī face Dardaniōs ferrōque sequāre colōnōs,
nunc, ōlim, quōcumque dabunt sē tempore vīrēs.
Lītora lītoribus contrāria, flūctibus undās
imprecor, arma armīs; pugnent ipsīque nepōtēsque."

1 **Tyriī**: Tyrians, citizens of Tyre who settled Carthage
stirps, stirpis, f., *stock*; refers to the Romans
2 **exercēte**: *harass*
odium, -ī, n., *hatred*
cinis, cineris, m., *ashes*
nostrō: = **meō**, with **cinerī**
3 **suntō**: *let there be*
4 **exorior, exorīrī, exortus sum**, *to rise up, arise*
Exoriāre: *Arise!* = **exoriāris**, present subjunctive
ultor, ultōris, m., *avenger*; a reference to Hannibal
5 **fax, facis**, f., *torch*
Dardanius, -a, -um, *Dardanian, Trojan*
sequāre: = **sequāris**, present subjunctive in relative clause of characteristic
colōnus, -ī, m., *colonist, settler*
6 **quīcumque, quaecumque, quodcumque**, *whoever, whatever*
vīrēs: from **vīs**, not **vir**
7 **contrārius, -a, -um** + dat., *against, opposed to*
flūctus, flūctūs, m., *water, sea*
unda, -ae, f., *wave; sea*
8 **imprecor, -ārī, -ātus sum**, *to pray*
nepōs, nepōtis, m., *descendant*

Name ________________________________ Date __________ Period ____________

Underline the correct answer.

1. Upon whom is Dido invoking hatred?

a. all peoples b. all future Romans c. her fellow Carthaginians d. the gods

2. In lines 2–3 there appears an example of

a. asyndeton b. chiasmus c. litotes d. synchysis

3. Dido prays that there be no love or ______ between the two nations.

a. common religion b. intermarriage c. treaty d. trade

4. In line 4, Dido asks that

a. she be allowed to avenge her death
b. someone arise from her ashes to avenge her
c. someone avenge her by burying her
d. she be allowed to return from the dead

5. The word **face** and **ferrō** (5) are examples of the figure

a. simile b. metonymy c. transferred epithet d. anaphora

6. The clause **quī . . . Dardaniōs . . . sequāre colōnōs** (5) is correctly translated

a. the Trojans who had followed as settlers
b. who in fact followed the Trojan settlers
c. whom the Trojan settlers might follow
d. who might follow the Trojan settlers

7. The relative pronoun **quī** (5) refers to

a. Dido b. Hannibal c. Aeneas d. the Trojan settlers

8. In lines 7–8, Dido prays for Carthage and Rome to fight

a. on land instead of on sea c. neither on land or sea
b. on land and sea d. only on Italian soil

9. Lines 7–8 contain

a. examples of ellipsis c. a pair of correlatives
b. nested clauses d. gapped verbs

10. What word is understood with **lītora, undās,** and **arma**?

a. **sunt** b. **et** c. **contrāria** d. **nec**

11. **Pugnent** (8) is best translated

a. let them fight b. they will fight c. they are fighting d. they must fight

12. By saying **ipsīque nepōtēsque** (8), the poet is implying

a. now and in the future c. all future time
b. past, present, and future d. sometime in the future

Name ______________________ Date ________ Period __________

CHAPTER 73

HORACE ON LIFE AND LOVE

Activity 73a Reading Skills: Horace's "Artful Joining"

Go Online PHSchool.com Web Code: jqd-0020

Given below are some nouns and pronouns from Reading 73A. Locate the adjective or participle that modifies each one and complete the puzzle.

ACROSS

1. tē (understood in line 10)
4. pariēs (14)
7. puer (1)
13. deōs (6)
14. simplex (5)
15. puer (1)
16. rosā (1)
18. quī (9
19. ventīs (7)
20. tabulā (13)

DOWN

1. tē (9)
2. puer (1)
3. tē (understood in line 10)
5. quī (11)
6. aequora (7)
8. comam (4)
9. puer (8)
10. vestīmenta (16)
11. odōribus (2)
12. aurae (12)
14. deō (16)
17. antrō (3)

Name ______________________ Date __________ Period __________

Activity 73b Writer's Techniques: More "Artful Joining"

1. Look at the relative placement of the words in Reading A, lines 1–3. How do the positions of the words contribute to your understanding of the meaning? Feel free to mark up the text below to illustrate your answer.

Quis multā gracilis tē puer in rosā

The words are placed relatively close to the way they would be placed in English which helps to translate and understand the sentence.

grātō, Pyrrha, sub antrō?

The commas help to differentiate the different phrases and the order is somewhat similar to english.

2. Look at the word order of **aspera nigrīs aequora ventīs** (6–7). What figure of speech does this illustrate? What effect does this word order have on the meaning?

This illustrates a violent wind and black sea. The word order doesn't affect the meaning.

3. For what reason is **tē** (9) in the ablative?

Because it is describing the second person.

4. Rewrite lines 10–11, filling in the words that are gapped:
quī semper vacuam, semper amābilem spērat.

Qui semper vacuam, semper amabilem sperat.

Name ______________________ Date __________ Period __________

5. Mē tabulā sacer

vōtīvā pariēs indicat ūvida

suspendisse potentī

vestīmenta maris deō.

a. In the lines above, draw an arrow from each adjective to the word that it modifies.

b. Write out this sentence in word order that better illustrates the fact that it contains an indirect statement.

____

____

Activity 73c Short Essay: Poetic Imagery

On separate paper, write a short essay in which you discuss how the poet uses the images of wind and water in Reading A. Support your observations by citing and translating appropriate Latin words and phrases.

Activity 73d Writer's Techniques: Contrast

In Reading B, Horace develops a vivid contrast in the first two stanzas. In a brief discussion, identify how Stanza 1 contrasts with Stanza 2. Be sure to cite relevant Latin words and phrases to support your observations.

____

____

____

____

____

____

____

Name ______________________________ Date __________ Period ____________

Activity 73e Meter: Alcaic

Reading B is written in the Alcaic meter, which was named after the Greek poet who wrote on the same theme used by Horace in this poem. Learn or review the pattern of this meter on page 310 in the textbook, then scan the following lines, and finally read aloud in correct meter.

Vidēs ut altā stet nive candidum

Sōracte nec iam sustineant onus

silvae labōrantēs gelūque

flūmina cōnstiterint acūtō?

Dissolve frīgus ligna super focō

largē repōnēns atque benignius

dēprōme quadrīmum Sabīnā,

ō Thaliarche, merum diōtā.

Activity 73f Language Skills: Sentence Structure in Poetry

1. Although Latin poetry, particularly that of Horace, is full of interesting poetic devices and images, the sentences contain the same basic structures with which you have become acquainted in reading prose, e.g., subordinate clauses, ablative absolutes, and participial phrases. Here below are lines 9–18 of Reading B written as prose. Do the following:

   Underline main clauses — Double underline subordinate clauses

   Squiggly underline participial phrases — Circle all imperatives

   Permitte dīvīs cētera, quī simul strāvēre ventōs aequore fervidō dēproeliantēs, nec cupressī nec veterēs agitantur ornī. Quid sit futūrum crās, fuge quaerere, et quem fors diērum cumque dabit, lucrō appōne nec dulcēs amōrēs sperne puer neque tū choreās, dōnec virentī cānitiēs abest mōrōsa.

2. What form is the verb **strāvēre**? How do you know?

   ____

Name ______________________ Date __________ Period ____________

Activity 73g Reading Skills: Recognizing What You See

A. Horace consistently uses details to illustrate generalized points that he is making. In Reading B, lines 18–24, he elaborates on the theme of young love. From these lines, copy out the Latin that corresponds to each English phrase. Do not include any extra words.

1. both the open spaces and the squares and the subdued whispers

   ____

2. now let (them) be sought out again ______________________________
3. at the arranged hour ______________________________
4. at nightfall ______________________________
5. the telltale (and) pleasing laughter ______________________________
6. of a girl hiding ______________________________
7. from the remotest corner ______________________________
8. and the love token torn away ______________________________
9. from the arm or from the finger ______________________________
10. resisting half-heartedly ______________________________

B. Locate and cite the example of onomatopoeia in these lines (see page 236 for review):

____

C. Find and cite the example of anaphora in these lines: ______________. In a single sentence, explain how the meaning, position, and repetition of this word contribute to the poet's message (cf. lines 14–18).

____

____

Name ______________________ Date __________ Period __________

Activity 73h Language Skills: Directing Someone to Do Something

A. In Reading C, the writer gives the girl to whom he is writing some strong advice. He expresses this in the form of prohibitions, direct commands, and gentle commands that express what is more like a suggestion. Copy out examples of each, then translate.

1. Prohibitions **a.** ______________________ trans. **a.** ______________________

b. ______________________ trans. **b.** ______________________

Such prohibitions are more often expressed as negative imperatives. Rewrite in that form.

a. ______________________

b. ______________________

2. Direct command ______________________ trans. ______________________

3. Gentle commands (with the subjunctive)

a. ______________________ trans. **a.** ______________________

b. ______________________ trans. **b.** ______________________

c. ______________________ trans. **c.** ______________________

Rewrite the gentle commands as regular imperatives.

a. ______________________

b. ______________________

c. ______________________

B. Translate the following sentence, which contains indirect commands:

Ego rogō ut diem carpās nēve posterō crēdās.

____

C. If the poet had wanted to insist that the girl was obligated to do what he was suggesting, e.g., *you must pick the day (like a flower)*, what grammatical construction would he have used? (See pages 148–149.) Use this construction to express the words in italics in Latin:

____

____

Name ______________________ Date __________ Period __________

Activity 73i Writer's Techniques: Poetic Imagery

Reading C contains several striking examples of imagery. Answer the following questions about each.

Image 1: How does the poet describe the passage of time in this poem? How is this image presented in a way that is unexpected? Include in your answer the specific Latin that provides the answers to these questions.

____

____

____

Image 2: What other image does the poet present to illustrate or clarify what he says? Write down the relevant Latin words and explain how each helps to develop this image.

____

____

____

Activity 73j Language Skills: Latin Word Order

Review the information about Latin word order on page 260 of the textbook. Choose the description that best matches each example and write its letter in the blank. Then rewrite the Latin using word order that is more common. The first one is done for you.

a. words spill to the left of their clause marker
b. first word in the clause is stressed
c. last word in the clause is stressed
d. word widely separated from its modifier/head word is stressed
e. relative pronoun appears before its antecedent

Example: Mē nunc Thressa Chloē regit (73D:9) *b*
Now Thracian Chloe rules me.

Nunc Thressa Chloē mē regit.

1. Haec cum dīxisset, prōcēdit extrā mūnitiōnēs. (60B:6) ______
When he had spoken these words, he progressed outside the fortifications.

____

2. Concussam bacchātur fāma per urbem. (72D:666) ______
The rumor runs wild through the shaken city.

____

(continued)

Name ______________________________ Date __________ Period ____________

3. Tantus amor necis est, querar ut cum Caesaris īrā. . . (71B:39) ______
There is such great love of death, that I find fault with Caesar's anger. . .

____

4. "Vīxī et quem dederat cursum fortuna perēgī. . ." (72D:653) ______
"I lived and completed the course that fortune had given . . ."

____

5. Mentem lymphātam Mareōticō redēgit in vērōs timōrēs Caesar. (68:14–16) ______
Caesar reduced to true fear(s) her mind deranged with Mareotic (wine).

____

6. Idem iste praetor monumenta . . . spoliāvit nūdāvitque omnia. (58A:14–16) ______
That very same man as governor plundered and stripped away all the most ancient monuments.

____

7. Quīque per autumnum percussīs frīgore prīmō est color in foliīs. . . (71B:29–30) ______
And the color which in autumn is in the leaves after being struck by the first cold. . .

____

8. Magna dīs immortālibus habenda est . . . grātia . . . (59C:1–2) ______
Great thanks must be given to the immortal gods . . .

____

9. Centuriōnēs ex eō, quō stābant, locō recessērunt. (60A:13) ______
The centurions withdrew from the place where they were stationed.

____

10. Errābant āctī fātīs maria omnia circum. (*Aeneid* 1.32) ______
Driven by the fates, they wandered about every sea.

____

11. Caesar, ab Ītaliā volantem (rēgīnam) rēmīs adurgēns, accipiter velut mollēs columbās (adurgēns). . . daret ut catēnīs fātāle mōnstrum. (68:16–21) ______ ______

Caesar, pursuing (the queen) closely with oars (ships) as she flew from Italy, just as a hawk (pursues) soft doves . . . so that he might place the destructive creature in chains.

____

____

Name ______________________ Date ________ Period __________

CHAPTER 74

OVID'S *METAMORPHOSES*

Go Online
PHSchool.com
Web Code: jqd-0021

Activity 74a Reading Skills: Participles and Gerunds

In lines 100–108 (up to **crēdēns***) of Reading A, locate, copy out, and write the line number of the following:*

1. a gerundive ____________ (modifies ____________)
2. a gerund and its direct object ____________
3. two present participles and the noun each modifies

   a. ____________ (modifies ____________)

   b. ____________ (modifies ____________)
4. an ablative absolute containing a perfect participle: ____________
5. two perfect participles used as substantives

   a. ____________ b. ____________
6. two future participles and the noun or pronoun each modifies

   a. ____________ (modifies ____________)

   b. ____________ (modifies ____________)

Activity 74b Writer's Techniques: Meter and Meaning

1. Mark the scansion of the following lines of dactylic hexameter (see page 311 of the textbook for help):

vixque sibī crēdēns, nōn altā fronde virentem

īlice dētrāxit virgam: virga aurea facta est;

tollit humō saxum: saxum quoque palluit aurō;

contigit et glaebam: contactū glaeba potentī

massa fit; ārentēs Cereris dēcerpsit aristās:

aurea messis erat; dēmptum tenet arbore pōmum:

Hesperidās dōnāsse putēs; sī postibus altīs

Name ______________________ Date __________ Period __________

admōvit digitōs, postēs radiāre videntur;

ille etiam liquidīs palmās ubi lāverat undīs,

unda fluēns palmīs Danaēn ēlūdere posset;

2. It is common to find a caesura in the third foot of a line of dactylic hexameter. Mark such caesurae with a raised double line // in the lines you scanned above. Excluding line 112, how many are there? ______

3. Line 112 might be considered to have a caesura in the third foot after **ārentēs**, but why would the reader probably not pause at that point?

____

4. What two lines contain a caesura, but not in the third foot? ______ ______

5. In which lines does the punctuation in your text reflect a break that coincides with a caesura (exclude line 112 again)?

____

6. In line 116, what adjective comes just before the caesura? ____________________
With what noun does this adjective agree? Where is this noun placed?

____

Watch out for more examples of this pattern, because Ovid does it frequently.

7. Even though there is no punctuation in line 117, how does caesura reflect the sentence structure?

____

8. Place a check mark next to the statements that are true about dactylic hexameter, based on what you have observed in this activity.

______ Caesurae very often indicate places where the reader might logically pause.

______ Caesurae always must come in the third foot.

______ Roman poets provided variety in their verse by putting pauses at different places in the line.

______ Roman poetry should be read mechanically, without thinking about the meaning.

______ Caesurae can help the reader know where phrases or clauses end.

9. Now practice reading these lines aloud with appropriate expression and pauses!

Name ______________________________ Date __________ Period ____________

Activity 74c Writer's Techniques: Change of Fortune

Answer the questions based on lines 121–130 of Reading B.

1. List three things (in both Latin and English) that Midas touches and tell what happens in each instance.

   a. Latin: ____________________ English: ____________________

   result: ____

   b. Latin: ____________________ English: ____________________

   result: ____

   c. Latin: ____________________ English: ____________________

   result: ____

2. What is Midas' mental state now? Cite the Latin for three things and translate each.

   a. ____

   b. ____

   c. ____

3. In what physical condition is Midas? Cite and translate the Latin for two things.

   a. ____

   b. ____

4. In lines 108–117, there is a similar list of things that Midas touched. How did Midas feel then (see lines 118–120)?

   ____

5. Why did Ovid include these two lists of things? How does including them help show what happens to Midas?

   ____

   ____

6. How does the word **invīsō** (130) summarize the change that Midas has undergone?

   ____

   ____

Name ______________________ Date __________ Period ____________

Activity 74d Reading Skills: Review

Select the item from the list on the right that matches the description on the left and write its letter in the blank. Not all answers will be used. Base your answers on lines 131–141 of Reading B.

______ **1.** a negative purpose clause		**a.** tuum . . . caput (140–141)
______ **2.** a participial phrase in the ablative		**b.** spūmigerō . . . fontī (140)
______ **3.** dative object of a compound verb		**c.** nē . . . maneās (136)
______ **4.** an example of ellipsis		**d.** peccāvimus (132)
______ **5.** dative case used with a compound adjective		**e.** lābentibus . . . undīs (138)
______ **6.** an example of hyperbaton		**f.** precor (133)
______ **7.** subjunctive verb in a clause introduced by *until*		**g.** miserēre (133)
______ **8.** 1st person plural that refers to only one person		**h.** peccāsse (134)
______ **9.** imperative of a deponent verb		**i.** mīte deum nūmen (134)
______ **10.** a syncopated verb		**j.** male optātō (136)
		l. veniās (139)

Activity 74e Reading Skills: Recognizing Phrases

Locate in Reading C and copy out the Latin that corresponds to the following English phrases. Do not include any extra words.

1. of the sacred mountain ______________________

2. of Midas alone ______________________

3. human shape ______________________

4. stupid ears ______________________

5. in(to) one part ______________________

6. with purple caps ______________________

7. accustomed to trim ______________________

8. the shame that had been seen ______________________

9. to the dug-up earth ______________________

10. he buries the evidence ______________________

11. from the filled-in trenches ______________________

12. a thick stand ______________________

13. by the gentle west wind ______________________

Activity 74f Reading Skills: Events in Order

The following sentences describe events that are mentioned in Reading D, but they are out of sequence. Write the numbers in the blanks below so that the sentences match the order of events given in the reading.

1. Opus patris puerī lūsū impedītus est.
2. Compositae pennae sunt similēs rūsticae fistulae.
3. Cēram pollice mollit puer rīdēns.
4. Daedalus pennās mediās līnō, īmās cērā iungit.
5. Daedalus ipse, cum opus cōnfēcisset, super terram ālīs suspendēbātur.
6. Aura pennās aliquās movēbat.
7. Ad locum nātālem redīre vult.
8. Per caelum, cum pateat, cōnstituit īre Daedalus.
9. Īcarus adest et pennās aurā mōtās captat.
10. Pennās in ōrdine, ā minimīs ad longissimās, pōnit.
11. Paulō flectit ālās quod vult eās esse similēs ālīs vērārum avium.
12. Rēx Mīnōs omnia praeter āera obstruit.
13. Daedalus īnsulam Crētam ōdit.
14. Daedalus artēs ignōtās temptat et nātūram mūtat.

Order: ______ ______ ______ ______ ______ ______ ______ ______ ______ ______

______ ______ ______ ______

Name ______________________________ Date __________ Period __________

Activity 74g Language Skills: Forwards and Backwards

Answer the following questions based on Reading E.

1. Locate three clauses whose words spill over to the left of the introductory word. Rewrite each clause in more common word order.

   a. ______________________________

   b. ______________________________

   c. ______________________________

   ____

2. Tell what noun each of the following modifies:

   a. mediō (203) ____________

   b. ignōtās (209) ____________

   c. senīlēs (210) ____________

   d. repetenda (212) ____________

   e. suō (212) ____________

   f. altō (213) ____________

   g. damnōsās (215) ____________

   h. suās, nātī (216) ____________

   i. tremulā (217) ____________

Activity 74h Reading Skills: Connections and Breaks

Base your answers to all questions in this activity on Reading F, lines 220–230.

1. Copy out the Latin that corresponds to the following English phrases. Do not include any extra words.

   a. Samos sacred to Juno ____________

   b. had been left behind ____________

   c. in (his) reckless flight ____________

   d. the pleasant-smelling wax ____________

   e. (his) bare arms ____________

   f. no breeze(s) ____________

   g. his mouth shouting ____________

2. In Activity 74b, you learned about the importance of caesurae in dactylic verse. Lines 220–230 all contain a caesura in the third foot that corresponds with a break in the sense (i.e., the beginning of a new phrase).

   a. In which lines does the punctuation in your text reflect the break in the sense? (Remember that ancient Roman readers did not have this assistance!)

   ____

   b. In which lines does the word **que** signal the beginning of a new phrase?

   ____

   c. In which lines does the caesura alone help the reader notice the break?

   ____

3. You also learned in Activity 74b that Ovid frequently connects a word at the end of the first half of the verse (just before the caesura) with a word at the very end of the line.

   a. In which line is a form of **esse** before the break completed by a past participle? ______

   b. In which lines does an adjective before the break modify a noun at the end of the line?

   ____

4. Practice reading lines 220–230 aloud. If necessary, write out the scansion on separate paper. However, if you have been practicing reading poetry carefully, you may find that you can read the lines reasonably well without writing out the scansion, especially since you know already that each of these lines has a caesura in the third foot.

Name ______________________________ Date __________ Period ____________

Activity 74i Sight Reading

Here is the story of Perdix, which comes immediately after the story of Icarus in Book VIII of the Metamorphoses. *Answer in English the questions that follow each section of the story. The middle portion is given in English translation.*

Hunc miserī tumulō pōnentem corpora nātī
garrula līmōsō prōspexit ab ēlice perdīx
et plausit pennīs testātaque gaudia cantū est,
ūnica tunc volucris nec vīsa priōribus annīs,
factaque nūper avis—longum tibi, Daedale, crīmen.

236 **Hunc:** = **Daedalum**
tumulō: = **sepulcrō**
237 **garrulus, -a, -um,** *talkative, chattering*
līmōsus, -a, -um, *muddy*
ēlix, ēlicis, m., *drainage ditch*
perdīx, perdīcis, f., *partridge (a bird)*
238 **plaudō, plaudere, plausī, plausus,** *to applaud*
testor, -ārī, -ātus sum, *to witness, bear witness (to)*
cantus, -ūs, m., *song, singing*
239 **volucris, volucris,** f., *winged creature, bird*
240 **longum:** in this context = *longlasting, longstanding*

1. What was Daedalus doing as the partridge watched him?

____

2. In what two ways did the partridge show its pleasure at what had happened to Daedalus?

a. ______________________________

b. ______________________________

3. Locate a poetic plural (see the Reading Note on page 280) in lines 236–238.

____

4. What are three things that we learn about the partridge in lines 239–240?

a. ______________________________

b. ______________________________

c. ______________________________

For his sister, ignorant of the fates, had handed over to this man (Daedalus) her son to be taught, a boy with twice six birthdays completed, with a mind ready for lessons; he also took the spine, noticed in the middle of a fish, as an example and cut a row of continuous teeth in sharp iron and discovered the use of the saw; he was the first to connect two iron legs from one joint, so that one part stood unmoving, when they were spread apart, and the other indicated a circle.

5. How old was Perdix when he was apprenticed to his uncle Daedalus?

____

6. What was the second thing that Perdix invented?

____

Daedalus invīdit sācrāque ex arce Minervae
praecipitem mīsit, lāpsum mentītus; at illum,
quae favet ingeniīs, excēpit Pallas avemque
reddidit et mediō vēlāvit in āere pennīs,
sed vigor ingeniī quondam vēlōcis in ālās
inque pedēs abiit; nōmen, quod et ante, remānsit.
Non tamen haec altē volucris sua corpora tollit,
nec facit in rāmīs altōque cacūmine nīdōs:
propter humum volitat pōnitque in saepibus ōva
antīquīque memor metuit sublīmia cāsūs.

250 **arx, arcis**, f., *citadel, fortress*
sācrā . . . arce Minervae: i.e, the Acropolis in Athens, a hill on which the temple of Athena (Minerva) stands
251 **mīsit**: supply **eum** (**Perdīcem**) as object of this and with **lāpsum**
praeceps, praecipitis, *headlong*
mentior, mentīrī, mentītus sum, *to lie, claim falsely*
253 **reddō, reddere, reddidī, redditus**, *to give back; to render, make*
vēlō, -āre, -āvī, -ātus, *to cover*
254 **quondam**: modifying **vēlōcis**, *formerly quick*
257 **cacūmen, cacūminis**, n., *peak*
nīdus, -ī, m, *nest*
258 **propter**: = **prope** in this context
volitō, -āre, -āvī, -ātus, *to fly, flutter*
saepes, saepis, f., *hedge*
259 **sublīmis, -is, -e**, *lofty, high*

Name ______________________ Date __________ Period __________

7. How did Daedalus feel after his nephew's talent showed itself?

____

8. What did Daedalus do in response to his feelings? How did he explain what happened?

____

____

9. How did Pallas Athena react? Why?

____

____

10. What happened to Perdix's talent? What part of him remained unchanged?

____

____

11. In lines 250–255, locate a relative pronoun that appears before its antecedent.

____

12. Name one thing that the partridge (unlike many other birds) does not do.

____

13. Name two behaviors typical of the partridge.

a. ____

b. ____

14. Why does it behave this way?

____

Name ______________________ Date ________ Period ____________

CHAPTER 75

THE MILLIONAIRE

Go Online
PHSchool.com
Web Code: jqd-0022

Activity 75a Language Skills: Recognizing What You See

In the grid below, you will find either a grammatical form or expression, a translation, or a grammatical identification. Fill in the missing information in the order in which it appears in Reading A.

Expression	Translation	Identification
	if a bad fate has overwhelmed them	
mē salvō (2)		
		result clause
cum ille . . . exemplar testāmentī iussit afferrī (5–6)		
	"getting down to business"	
ingemēscente familiā (6)		
		present participle
amīce cārissime (7)		
ut . . . pingās (8–9)		
	so that it may befall me	
volō (ut) sint (11)		subjunctive with a wish
vīvō . . . esse (12)		
diūtius (13)		
		passive periphrastic with dative of agent
adicī (13)		
		jussive (independent) subjunctive

Name ______________________ Date __________ Period __________

Activity 75b Language Skills: Trimalchio's Latin I

Answer each question as directed.

1. The following sentence contains two illustrations of Trimalchio's use of shaky Latin. Circle the offending words and correct them.

   Trimalchiō, "Amīcī," inquit, "et servī hominēs sunt et aequē ūnum lactem bibērunt, etiam sī illōs malus fātus oppresserit. (1–2)

   Correction 1 ______________ Correction 2 ______________

2. Trimalchio frequently uses what are known as colloquial, or everyday, expressions in his speech. One of these is **ad summum** in line 3. What is the figurative meaning of this phrase?

   ____

3. On page 35 of the textbook, you learned that a participial phrase can be nested inside the main clause or a subordinate clause. In this sentence from Reading A, underline the subordinate clause once and the nested participial phrase twice.

   Grātiās agere omnēs indulgentiae coeperant dominī, cum ille oblītus nūgārum exemplar testāmentī iussit afferrī. (5–6)

4. What is the unexpressed subject of **inquit** in line 7? ______________

5. The word that introduces the clause **ut sint** (10) is gapped. What is it? ______________

Activity 75c Language Skills: Participles

In the first paragraph of Reading B, there are six present participles and three past participles. List each and the word it modifies in the spaces provided.

Present Participle	Word Modified	Past Participle	Word Modified
______	______	______	______
______	______	______	______
______	______	______	______
______	______		
______	______		
______	______		

Name ______________________ Date __________ Period ____________

Activity 75d Language Skills: Transformation

In each of the following activities, you are asked to transform one expression into another. Some variation in word order is permitted.

1. Write in Latin the direct command from which the indirect command **ut . . . euntēs** (15) is derived.

   ____

2. Trimalchio uses a colloquialism in expressing the indirect statement in line 17: **scīs enim, quod epulum dedī, bīnōs dēnāriōs**. Express this in correct literary Latin.

   ____

3. Transform the **ut** purpose clause in line 22 into a gerundive of purpose.

   ____

4. Transform the main clause **et urnam licet frāctam sculpās** (21) so that **licet** is followed by an infinitive instead of a subjunctive. For the past participle, substitute a relative clause.

   ____

5. Write the following sentence in Latin, using a relative clause of characteristic. Use the vocabulary in Reading B.

   Let Habinnas carve an amphora of the sort from which wine may not spill out.

   ____

6. Using the concessive clause **cum posset** (24–25) as a model, write in Latin the following sentence.

   Although Trimalchio had lived (as) a poor man, nevertheless he did not die (as) a poor man.
   (poor man = **pauper, pauperis**, adjective used as a substantive)

   ____

   ____

Activity 75e Reading Skills: Using Your Imagination

On a separate piece of unlined paper, draw a sketch of Trimalchio's tomb, as you imagine it from the descriptions in Readings A and B. Be sure to include the epitaph in Latin, lines 23–26. Don't worry if you "can't draw;" do your best!

Name ______________________ Date __________ Period ____________

Activity 75f Reading Skills: Sequencing Thoughts

Below you will find nine modified sentences from Reading B that describe Trimalchio's rise to fame and fortune. Put them in the sequence in which they occurred in the storyline by writing 1 (happened first), 2 (second), etc., in the spaces provided.

1. Cum nāvēs dēlētae erant, tamen Trimalchiō nōn dēfēcit.
2. Trimalchiō domum et fundōs patrōnī suī ēmit.
3. Nāvibus aedificātīs, Trimalchiō vīnum onerāvit.
4. Volēbat, cum nēmō umquam satis habēret, negōtium suscipere.
5. Trimalchiō servus dominus in domō factus est.
6. Uxor Trimalchiōnis, omnibus vestīmentīs vēnditīs, eī aureōs dedit.
7. Cum cohērēs Caesarī factus esset, ā dominō mortuō plūrimam pecūniam accēpit.
8. Holera, unguenta, servōs in maiōribus nāvibus onerāvit.
9. Ūnō diē omnēs nāvēs suae naufragārunt.

_____ _____ _____ _____ _____ _____ _____ _____ _____

Activity 75g Trimalchio's Latin II

In Reading C, find and write in the spaces provided an example of each form or expression, or answer the question, as appropriate.

1. A syncopated verb ______________________
2. A noun used with incorrect gender ______________________
3. A Latin synonym for the colloquial expression **ad summum**

   ____
4. A pair of correlatives ______________________
5. A simile ______________________
6. Explain the imagery in **Neptūnus trecentiēs sēstertium dēvorāvit.** (8–9)

   ____

   ____
7. Of what figure of speech is the following an example? **Onerāvī rūrsus vīnum, lardum, fabam, sēplasium, manicipia.** (12)

   ____

Name ______________________ Date __________ Period ____________

Activity 75h Reading Skills: Analysis

Briefly discuss the aspect of Trimalchio's character or personality illustrated by the following excerpts from several of the readings in this chapter. Support your observations by selecting, citing, and translating relevant words or phrases from the Latin provided below.

1. Tē rogō ut . . . faciās . . . mē in tribūnālī sedentem praetextātum cum ānulīs aureīs quinque et nummōs in pūblicō dē sacculō effundentem. (B:15–16)

2. Hōrologium in mediō (sit), ut quisquis hōrās īnspiciet, velit nōlit, nōmen meum legat. (B:21–22)

3. Aedificāvī hanc domum. Ut scītis, casula erat; nunc templum est. Habet quattuor cēnātiōnēs, cubicula vīgintī, porticūs marmorātōs duōs . . . . (D:24–26)

4. Crēdite mihi; assem habeās, assem valeās; habēs, habēberis. Sīc amīcus vester, quī fuit rāna, nunc est rēx. (D:30)

____

____

____

____

____

____

____

Activity 75i Reading Skills: Everyday Latin

Match Trimalchio's colloquial or everyday expressions with their meanings.

______ 1. ab aciā et acū (D:22)

______ 2. quī fuit rāna, nunc est rēx (D:30)

______ 3. intestīnās meās noverat (D:22)

______ 4. manum dē tābulā (D:18)

______ 5. crēscēbat tamquam favus (C:16–17)

______ 6. mi haec iactūra gustī fuit (C:9–10)

______ 7. factum, nōn fābula (C:8)

______ 8. contrā aurum (C:7)

______ 9. Nē multīs vōs morer (C:6)

______ 10. velit nōlit (B:22)

a. (I took my) hand off the tablet

b. fact, not fiction

c. it grew like a honeycomb

d. whether he wants to or not

e. to make a long story short

f. worth its weight in gold

g. from thread to needle

h. this loss was worth a tiny bit

i. he knew my guts

j. he who was a frog is now a king

Name ______________________________ Date __________ Period __________

Activity 75j Sight Reading

Cavē canem! *An accident occurs to several of Trimalchio's dinner guests, who had been contemplating a bath.*

Cum haec placuissent, dūcente per porticum Gitone ad iānuam vēnimus, ubi canis catēnārius tantō nōs tumultū excēpit, ut Ascyltos etiam in piscīnam ceciderit. Nec nōn ego quoque ēbrius, quī etiam pictum timueram canem, dum natantī opem ferō, in eundem gurgitem tractus sum. Servāvit nōs tamen ātriēnsis, quī interventū suō et canem plācāvit et nōs trementēs extrāxit in siccum. Et Gitōn quidem iam dūdum sē ratiōne acūtissimā redēmerat ā cane; quicquid enim ā nōbīs accēperat dē cēnā, lātrantī sparserat, ille āvocātus cibō furōrem suppresserat.

—Petronius, *Satyricon* (extract)

1 **Cum haec placuissent**: *Since this was agreeable*
Gitōn, Gitonis, m., one of the characters in the story
catēnārius, -a, -um, *chained*
2 **Ascyltos, -ī**, m., another character
nec nōn, *likewise, and also*
3 **pingō, pingere, pīnxī, pictus**, *to paint*
natō, -āre, -āvī, -ātus, *to swim*
ops, opis, f., *help, aid*
gurgēs, gurgitis, m., *abyss, depths*; epic exaggeration
4 **ātriēnsis, ātriēnsis**, m., *porter, steward*
interventus, -ūs, m., *intervention*
5 **siccus, -a, -um**, *dry*; substantive, *dry land*
iam dūdum, adv., *long ago*
ratiō, ratiōnis, f., *plan, scheme*
acūtus, -a, -um, *sharp, clever*
redimō, redimere, redēmī, redēmptus, *to ransom, redeem*
6 **lātrantī**: = **lātrantī canī**
spargō, spargere, sparsī, sparsus, *to scatter*
ille: = **canis**

Mark each statement ***V (Vērum)*** *or* ***F (Falsum)***:

______ **1.** The narrator led Giton through the portico to the doorway.

______ **2.** A chained-up dog created a commotion.

______ **3.** Ascyltos fell into the fishpond because he was drunk.

______ **4.** The narrator had earlier been afraid of a picture of a dog.

______ **5.** The narrator jumped in because he could swim.

______ **6.** The steward summoned help.

______ **7.** Now calm, the dog pulled the guests out of the water.

______ **8.** The guests were trembling when they reached dry land.

______ **9.** Giton's plan had been to win over the dog with food from dinner.

______ **10.** The plan did not work but only enraged the dog further.

Name ______________________ Date ________ Period ___________

CHAPTER 76

DEATH OF PLINY THE ELDER

Go Online PHSchool.com Web Code: jqd-0023

Activity 76a Writer's Techniques: Tenses of Verbs

In his letter, Pliny uses the historical present (review the Reading Note on page 61 if needed) along with regular past tenses (perfect, imperfect, pluperfect). From Reading A, copy out all examples of the following tenses, both indicative and subjunctive (do not include infinitives), in the order in which they are found and then answer the questions that follow.

Historical Present	Imperfect	Perfect	Pluperfect
___________	___________	___________	___________
___________	___________	___________	___________
___________	___________	___________	___________
___________	___________	___________	
___________	___________		
___________	___________		
___________	___________		
___________	___________		
___________	___________		
___________	___________		
___________	___________		
___________	___________		
	___________		

1. What tense is used for actions that were going on continuously or as a backdrop to actions taken by Pliny the Elder? ___________

2. What tense is used for the actions that Pliny the Elder took in response to the crisis?

____

3. Why did Pliny the Younger put a few events in the perfect rather than the historical present?

____

____

____

Activity 76b Writer's Techniques: Fast-moving Narrative

Pliny the Younger uses several techniques to keep the narrative moving quickly. In Reading A locate and copy out examples of the following (they occur in this order in the reading):

1. substantives (2) a. ______________________

   b. ______________________

2. ellipsis (2) a. ______________________

   b. ______________________

3. gapping ______________________

4. asyndeton (3) a. ______________________

   b. ______________________

   c. ______________________

Ellipsis, gapping, and asyndeton all involve the omission of words, which makes them useful figures of speech when a writer wants to construct a fast-moving narrative. In what way is the use of substantives similar?

____

____

____

Name ____ Date __________ Period ____________

Activity 76c Reading Skills: Recognizing What You See

Complete the grid below, based on Reading B. Remember to indent the Latin items appropriately, keeping main clauses at the left margin.

	main clause begins
	relative clause
	main clause ends
	another main clause
	participial phrase with two participles
	main clause ends, verb is gapped
	another main clause, ellipsis of verb
	participial phrase
	indirect question
	main clause begins
	indirect command
	main clause resumes (one word)
	direct quotation begins
	main verb
	direct quotation ends (two parts)
	another main clause
	new main clause begins (one word)
	ablative absolute begins
	cum clause
	ablative absolute ends
	main clause resumes
	conditional clause
	participial phrase
	main clause; three verbs in asyndeton
	another main clause starts (one word)
	purpose clause
	main clause ends
	main clause; two verbs in asyndeton
	adjectival phrases describing subject

Name ______________________________ Date __________ Period __________

Activity 76d Writer's Techniques: Narrative/Expository Writing in Latin

Reading C contains dramatic passages describing the effect of the eruption of Vesuvius on Pliny the Elder and the others who were staying at Pomponianus' villa. Give a close paraphrase of the Latin describing each of the following events; then place them in the sequence in which they happened by writing the numbers in the blanks at the bottom.

1. cervīcālia capitibus imposita linteīs cōnstringunt

____

2. nunc hūc nunc illūc abīre aut referrī vidēbantur

____

3. nam crēbrīs vāstīsque tremōribus tēcta nūtābant

____

4. interim ē Vesuviō monte plūrimīs locīs lātissimae flammae altaque incendia relūcēbant

____

5. levium exēsōrumque pūmicum cāsus metuēbātur

____

6. sed ārea . . . iam cinere mixtīsque pūmicibus opplēta surrēxerat

____

7. quasi ēmōta sēdibus suīs

____

8. in commūne cōnsultant (utrum) intrā tēcta subsistant an in apertō vagentur

____

9. Plīnius agrestium trepidātiōne ignēs relictōs dēsertāsque vīllās per sōlitūdinem ardēre . . . dictitābat

____

____

Order:

_____ _____ _____ _____ _____ _____ _____ _____ _____

Name ______________________________ Date __________ Period __________

Activity 76e Language Skills: Pronoun Review

Locate each of the following pronouns in Readings C and D and then identify the word to which each pronoun refers by writing it in the column at the right. For relative pronouns, include a translation of the antecedent.

Pronoun	Reference / antecedent
quōrum (26)	
quī (29)	
illī (29)	
quī (29)	
quā (31)	
sē (32)	
quī (33)	
illum (37)	
id (38)	
quam (40)	
quod (42)	
illum (45	
illī (46)	
is (47)	
eō (47)	
quem (47)	

How do you know that **quam** (49) is not a relative pronoun?

____

____

Name ______________________ Date __________ Period __________

Activity 76f Reading Skills

Write the Latin for each of the following, based on Reading D.

1. the odor of sulphur, portending fire

____

2. It was decided to go out onto the shore

____

3. Leaning on two small slaves

____

4. a night thicker and blacker than all nights

____

5. lying on a cloth spread out (on the ground)

____

6. with his windpipe closed

____

7. more like a person asleep than a dead person

____

Activity 76g Writer's Techniques: Stated and Unstated

Sometimes writers do not state things explicitly; instead, they leave it to the reader to notice what is omitted and to draw appropriate conclusions.

1. In the sentence that begins **Ibi** (42) we learn two things; what are they?

   a. ____

   b. ____

2. What effect did the flames and the odor of sulphur have on Pliny the Elder, as compared with others in the group?

____

(continued)

3. What do these things tell us about Pliny the Elder's condition, even though his nephew does not specifically say it?

____

____

4. Who was left with Pliny the Elder at this point? Why?

____

____

5. Pliny the Younger does not make any comment about the fact that his uncle had been abandoned by his friends. Why do you think they behaved as they did? Would such an action have been justified? Why does Pliny not comment on their behavior?

____

____

____

____

____

____

____

Activity 76h Pompeii: You are There

After completing Reading D and contemplating the picture on page 305 of your text, write in English on separate paper a creative story in which you pretend you are one of the two young slaves mentioned in line 45. Using the details provided in Reading D, describe what you see, hear, smell, and experience during the death of Pliny the Elder.